I0032082

Revolutionize Service Industry Hiring: Innovative Strategies for Exceptional Results

Leveraging AI and Data in Recruitment

Wells Ye

© **Copyright 2024 - All rights reserved.**

The content contained within this book may not be reproduced, duplicated or transmitted without direct written permission from the author or the publisher.

Under no circumstances will any blame or legal responsibility be held against the publisher, or author, for any damages, reparation, or monetary loss due to the information contained within this book, either directly or indirectly.

Legal Notice:

This book is copyright protected. It is only for personal use. You cannot amend, distribute, sell, use, quote or paraphrase any part, or the content within this book, without the consent of the author or publisher.

Disclaimer Notice:

Please note the information contained within this document is for educational and entertainment purposes only. All effort has been executed to present accurate, up to date, reliable, complete information. No warranties of any kind are declared or implied. Readers acknowledge that the author is not engaged in the rendering of legal, financial, medical or professional advice. The content within this book has been derived from various sources. Please consult a licensed professional before attempting any techniques outlined in this book.

By reading this document, the reader agrees that under no circumstances is the author responsible for any losses, direct or indirect, that are incurred as a result of the use of the information contained within this document, including, but not limited to, errors, omissions, or inaccuracies.

Table of Contents

Chapter 1:

The Recruitment Quagmire—

Overwhelmed and Understaffed

You sit at your desk, staring at the 81st application of the day, each blending into the next. It's a sea of resumes from overqualified, underqualified, and questionably qualified candidates. Your phone buzzes with another urgent email from management: "We need those roles filled ASAP!" Meanwhile, your coffee's gone cold, and you're only halfway through the applicant list. You wonder if you'll have to start pulling resumes from a hat. Somewhere, another trainee just quit mid-training.

It's chaos, and you're at the center of it all.

Now, with demand outpacing supply, let's talk about why finding more staff has become mission-critical.

The Dire Need for More Staff

The service industry refers to businesses that provide intangible goods and services rather than physical products. This sector includes various companies that support daily operations and consumer needs, often involving customer interaction and maintenance of essential functions.

The demand for workers in the service industry remains consistently high because these roles are crucial to the smooth running of everyday business operations. With enough staff, businesses in this sector can function efficiently, leading to customer service and productivity disruptions.

Examples of service industries include

- **Maid services:** These are businesses or individuals offering regular or one-time cleaning and housekeeping services to residential clients. They focus on tasks like dusting, vacuuming, and sanitizing surfaces. Often customizable, these services are convenient for busy households or those needing additional support.

- **Commercial cleaning:** These companies specialize in cleaning nonresidential spaces like office buildings, schools, and hospitals, ensuring these environments remain sanitary and safe for occupants. Services often include deep cleaning, floor maintenance, and waste management to meet industry regulations.

- **Restaurants:** From fast-food and casual eateries to fine dining establishments, restaurants offer prepared meals and beverages for on-site dining or takeout. They provide diverse cuisine, unique atmospheres, and various service styles, strongly impacting local and global economies.

- **Retail stores:** These businesses provide consumers with direct access to goods, offering everything from clothing and electronics to groceries and household items for a convenient shopping experience. Retail stores may operate in physical locations or online, aiming to meet diverse consumer needs.

- **Caregivers:** Professionals in caregiving provide essential support to individuals with varying needs, from daily assistance to medical care, improving quality of life. They often serve children, people with disabilities, or elderly clients in their homes or through specialized facilities.

- **Security services:** These companies offer protection through trained personnel and surveillance systems, securing properties and people. Security services provide on-site guards, alarm systems, and monitoring to prevent unauthorized access and keep people and properties safe.

- **Call centers:** Call centers handle customer service, technical support, and sales inquiries through phone, chat, or email, often serving as the front line for client interactions. They provide real-time support and efficiently resolve issues to help businesses maintain strong customer relationships.

These roles are the backbone of many businesses, enabling them to meet customer demands and sustain operational efficiency. Maintaining adequate staffing levels in the service industry is critical with such broad and essential functions.

The hospitality sector faced a staggering turnover rate of about 73.8% in 2023, showing how tough it is to keep a stable workforce (The Importance of Employee Retention, 2023). Also, in 2023, the restaurant industry faced a significant staffing challenge, with workforce levels 3.6% lower than before the pandemic, according to data from the National Restaurant Association (Jones, n.d.). This gap equates to about 450,000 job vacancies compared to 2019. Additionally, 62% of restaurant operators reported being unable to hire enough staff to meet customer demand. In comparison, 80% struggled to fill available roles).

As HR recruiters, small business owners, or HR leaders, you might find yourself trapped in an endless cycle of staff replacement, especially since the service industry in general is the largest sector of the global economy.

The challenge isn't just about filling vacant positions—it's about doing it quickly to avoid or reduce revenue loss. If a restaurant is understaffed, it might have to turn customers away or limit seating, which hits immediate sales and can hurt customer loyalty in the long run. According to Clinton Anderson, CEO of Fourth, restaurants generally experience a loss of 10%–25% in gross revenue per location when they cannot adequately staff to meet demand (Gansser, 2023).

When customers face long wait times or receive poor service due to staffing shortages, they will likely take their business elsewhere, impacting your growth over time. When management pressures you to hire faster, especially while you're competing with other companies that might offer slightly better pay or perks, the urgency ramps up even more.

Adding to the problem is the burnout your current staff might be experiencing. When roles remain unfilled, the existing employees must pick up the slack, leading to fatigue and frustration. This is especially troublesome in industries like caregiving, where nearly half the workforce reported burnout during the pandemic. But it's not just a care sector issue—burnout is becoming more common across all service sectors. According to EmployJoy.ai recruiting data, in 2023, 25% of job applicants for maid services list burnout as the top reason for leaving their last job.

As employees feel overwhelmed and unsupported, they're more likely to leave, increasing turnover rates even further. This affects team morale and puts extra pressure on you to fill more positions. All these factors contribute to a vicious cycle that's hard to break.

The diagram below illustrates the vicious recruiting cycle, starting from the need for more staff.

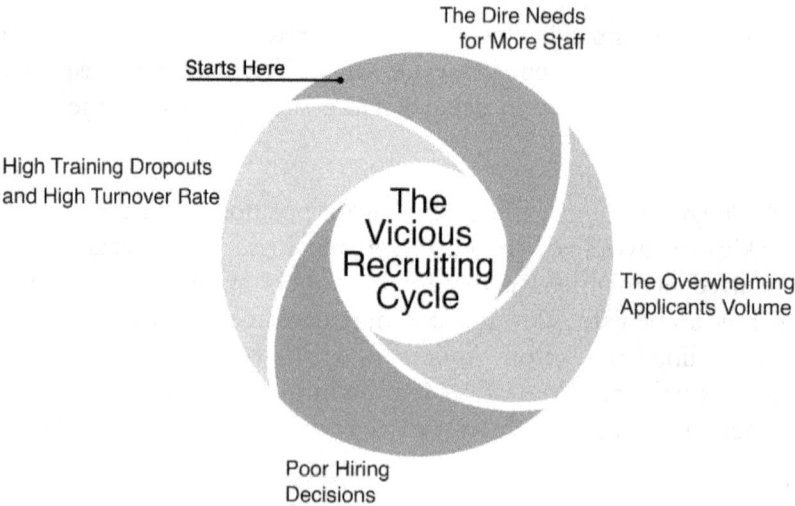

The Dire Needs
for More Staff

Starts Here

High Training Dropouts
and High Turnover Rate

The
Vicious
Recruiting
Cycle

The Overwhelming
Applicants Volume

Poor Hiring
Decisions

It's a recruiting nightmare. Gallup reported that turnover could cost up to twice an employee's salary when considering the expenses involved in recruiting, training, and the opportunity costs of unfilled positions (McFeely & Wigert, 2019). These expenses can quickly add up and sap your budget and resources.

Moreover, the financial impact isn't limited to the obvious expenses and revenue loss due to staffing issues. There are hidden costs like overtime pay for remaining staff, decreased productivity due to overworked employees, and potential mistakes or accidents resulting from fatigue. These problems can result in consumer discontent, damaging reviews, and legal issues. All of this adds another layer of complexity to your already challenging role in recruitment.

Competing for talent adds yet another hurdle. With so many businesses in the service industry facing similar staffing challenges, the competition to attract and retain quality employees is fierce. You're not only trying to fill positions quickly but also aiming to stand out as an employer of choice. This might involve offering competitive salaries, better benefits, or more flexible work schedules—all of which can stretch your company's resources thin. It's a tricky balance between meeting your staffing needs and maintaining your bottom line.

Understanding how internal turnover amplifies pressure on your recruitment process is crucial. Let's focus on how the loss of seasoned employees makes these challenges even more significant.

Internal Turnover Amplifying Pressure on Employees

When you're facing internal staff shortages, your recruitment processes can get seriously disrupted, causing a ripple effect throughout your organization. A spike in turnover rates means your existing employees must pick up the slack, often juggling multiple extra duties that stretch them thin. This mounting pressure can quickly spiral into burnout, dragging down both morale and productivity across the board.

Mistakes become more frequent as your team is overworked, leading to costly operational slowdowns. Suddenly, you're facing more than just empty seats—financial setbacks and hits to your reputation begin to loom on the horizon.

High turnover doesn't just strain your resources; it also shakes up your team dynamics in a big way. Every time someone exits, your team has to adapt to new faces, which disrupts the consistency of workflows and can throw long-term projects off course. Constantly needing to onboard new employees drains time and energy you could better spend on driving growth or sparking innovation. Instead of honing their skills and advancing in their roles, your team members find themselves stuck in a loop of retraining newcomers. Both trainers and managers find this incredibly frustrating. Trainers might feel they're wasting their efforts, and managers are eager to see progress instead of constantly playing catch-up.

Here's a sample computation of the total cost of turnover:

Category	Amount	Note
Recruiting Cost	$4,700	SHRM, Society for Human Resource Management
Revenue Loss - Opportunity Cost	$6,000	Assuming recruiting and training time of 1 month and a daily revenue impact of $300
Training Cost	$1,096	https://trainingmag.com/, average training cost for a small company.
Cost of the Time to Full Productivity	$6,240	Assuming it takes the average new employee two month to fully onboard and fully productive. Assuming a fully loaded hourly pay rate of $19.5 per hour.
Total Cost of Turnover	$18,036	

Don't forget about the financial strain. (Please see the total cost of turnover in the above table.) Costs for recruiting, training, and productivity loss all affect your budget. In industries like healthcare and hospitality, where turnover can rack up millions in yearly expenses, these losses pile up fast. Companies that can't keep their employees often face a domino effect of operational setbacks. The Chartered Institute of Personnel and Development highlights that employee retention is a significant worry, emphasizing that prioritizing retention strategies is crucial to keeping these escalating costs in check (*Resourcing and Talent*, 2022).

One clear takeaway from the data is that opportunity costs comprise 33.27% of turnover expenses, primarily due to revenue loss and the time required to reach total productivity.

Finally, the nonstop pressure to recruit can weaken your company's competitive edge, leaving less budget for substantial investments like technology upgrades or employee development programs. Spinning to handle the crisis becomes the overwhelming priority, sidelining all other initiatives. Over time, this cycle can harm your company's reputation, making attracting and keeping top talent down the line more challenging. Even your relationships with customers can take a hit if they pick up on the instability, especially in industries that depend on consistent and reliable service. Suppose clients sense that your team is constantly changing or overwhelmed. In that case, they might start looking elsewhere, affecting your bottom line further.

The COVID-19 pandemic caused labor shortages, intensifying all these challenges. The pandemic dramatically reshaped the recruitment landscape, making understanding and addressing these shortages more critical.

Severe Labor Shortage Due to the Pandemic

Before COVID-19, finding adequate staff was already a challenge. Still, the widespread furloughs and layoffs during the pandemic made things even worse. Strict lockdowns and reduced customer demand especially hurt the hospitality and retail sectors.

At the same time, many potential candidates were hesitant to return to these roles because they were concerned about health and safety. Jobs that involved close contact with customers—like food service and retail—carried a higher risk of COVID-19 exposure. Understandably, many former workers are reluctant to return to these fields, which shrinks the talent pool further.

Another factor is that many people who used to work in the service industry have moved on to different sectors or adapted to remote work. As some businesses shifted online during the pandemic, there was a surge in demand for remote and tech-driven roles. These positions offer safety, flexibility, and sometimes better pay than traditional service industry jobs. As a result, you now have an even smaller pool of workers to recruit.

Effects of Fierce Competition

In a tight job market, attracting top talent means standing out among fierce competition. As you face a shortage of skilled candidates, enhancing job offers with higher wages, better benefits, and flexible working conditions becomes crucial—yet this also puts pressure on balancing those appealing offers with budget limitations.

The Growing Challenge of Retaining Current Employees

The pressure isn't limited to attracting new talent; retaining your current staff becomes equally challenging. High turnover rates demand more time, money, and resources to constantly hire and train new employees. This exhausting cycle hampers your ability to build a stable and experienced workforce. If unaddressed, the constant flux can destabilize your team, increase workloads, and lower overall morale and productivity.

Service Reductions and Shortened Hours as a Response to Staffing Struggles

Recognizing that these staffing challenges are part of a more significant industry-wide issue is essential. Many businesses have had to reduce services, limit operating hours, or close for a time because they need more staff. These cutbacks hurt your ability to recruit and retain talent and have a broader impact on the economy and customer satisfaction. Reduced services can lead to fewer opportunities for growth and innovation in the service industry.

Hiring Under Pressure: Increased Risk of Mistakes and Turnover

The talent shortage has put enormous pressure on recruiters to fill positions quickly, which can lead to rushed hiring decisions. Lowering standards, cutting corners during interviews, or hiring ill-suited candidates can backfire, leading to higher turnover rates. This creates a vicious cycle where mistakes made during the hiring process result in further staff shortages, increasing the strain on remaining employees and exacerbating turnover. This constant pressure can lead to burnout for recruiters and the staff they're trying to retain.

All these factors contribute to a challenging environment where traditional recruitment strategies might not be as effective as they once were. You're in unfamiliar territory, and deciding the proper course can feel overwhelming.

Now that we've covered the pressing need for more staff and how the pandemic has wholly reshaped the labor market, it's time to look at another surprising aspect of this situation. Although you have trouble finding suitable candidates, you might still receive many applications. It seems contradictory—why are you getting so many applications when the labor pool is shrinking? Let's get to the bottom of this overwhelming influx of applicants.

The Overwhelming Applicant Pool

The service industry faces a unique recruitment challenge: Low barriers to entry attract a flood of applicants, but not necessarily the right ones. This mismatch, combined with the demands of managing high volumes of candidates, complicates hiring efforts and strains already thin-stretched teams.

Low Barriers of Entry Always Result in Higher Volume

Suppose you're scratching your head over why there's a flood of applicants for service industry jobs despite a labor shortage. In that case, it's mainly because these roles have such low barriers to entry. Jobs in hospitality, retail, and customer service generally don't ask for much in terms of educational and experience qualifications. Since these positions don't need specialized skills or advanced education, almost anyone can throw their name into the hat—from high school grads to folks hunting for a part-time gig. The result? Applications flood in and overwhelm you.

Impact of Labor Shortage

Does a high volume of applicants contradict the concept of a labor shortage during the pandemic?

The answer is no.

Because of low barriers to entry, there are always waves of applicants for service industry roles. However, during the pandemic-induced labor shortage, those waves have been smaller, though still considerable. The shortage pushed some workers to switch careers or leave the workforce temporarily, leading to fewer applications than usual. However, hiring managers still sorted through more applications than they could manage. The mismatch between available workers and industry demands resulted in a chaotic hiring landscape where employers struggled to fill roles yet remained swamped by a reduced but steady flow of candidates.

In short, it's still a flood—just a smaller one with fewer quality applicants!

These jobs—whether you're talking about being a cashier, a server, or a front-desk clerk—typically require basic customer service abilities, a friendly demeanor, and sometimes just the physical ability to stand for extended periods. Because of this, you get applicants who are overqualified, underqualified, or simply in need of immediate employment. While that might seem like a bonus at first glance, this wide-open door brings unique challenges for you as a recruiter.

According to the SHRM, recruiters spend about 23 hours screening resumes for just 1 hire, which only multiplies when dealing with such high volumes (McNeel, 2024). This can be especially tough when you're already short on staff and feeling stretched thin.

Moreover, only some applicants bring the necessary skills or experience, even for these seemingly straightforward jobs. Sure, these positions might not require a college degree. However, essential skills like problem-solving, effective communication, and basic computer literacy are still crucial. Finding candidates with these qualities— without burning out your existing team—is a real challenge. Take, for instance, someone who applies for a customer service role just because it doesn't need formal qualifications; if they lack patience or people skills, they're not exactly a great fit.

Mismatch of Qualifications

This mismatch between applicants and job requirements adds extra time and complexity to your hiring process. You end up sifting through piles of resumes to find a handful that might be worth considering. And it's not just a time suck; it can bog down your entire hiring timeline. Glassdoor reports that hiring in the US typically takes 23 days (*Interview Process*, 2015). Still, having too many applicants can make that timeline stretch out even longer. In the meantime, positions stay vacant, forcing your current staff to pick up the slack, which can lead to burnout and even higher turnover rates.

Imagine you're recruiting for a well-known restaurant chain. You're looking to fill multiple positions that require minimal qualifications— maybe just a high school diploma and some experience in customer service. Because the job market is tight, hundreds of applications inundate you. Some candidates are overqualified, while others don't even have essential basic skills, not to mention restaurant experience. It's a double-edged sword: You've got many candidates to sort through, but only a few are genuinely suitable for the roles.

So, you face a challenging situation. The low entry barriers of service industry jobs lead to many applicants, but not necessarily the right ones. The sheer volume makes the hiring process longer and more complicated, putting extra strain on your team and potentially impacting your business operations.

Key Takeaways

- Recruiters in the service industry grapple with high turnover and labor shortages, which push them to fill roles swiftly to avoid hits to customer service and revenue. This urgency can lead to hiring compromises, as the pressure to keep operations running is often relentless.

- Unfilled roles lead to an added workload on current employees, causing burnout and further turnover that drains company resources and morale. This cycle strains budgets and makes it even harder to stabilize teams long-term, impacting the overall work environment.

- The COVID-19 pandemic intensified these recruitment hurdles by introducing health risks and accelerating a shift toward remote work, shrinking the available labor pool. Many workers have chosen alternative industries or remote roles, reducing the number of candidates willing to work in-person service jobs.

- Low barriers to entry in these roles draw in a flood of applicants. Still, many lack the necessary skills, complicating the hiring process. Sorting through these applications takes more time and effort, leading to longer timelines for identifying qualified candidates.

- The high volume of applicants often results in qualification mismatches, making it difficult to pinpoint the right fit without slowing hiring. This challenge requires a careful balance between filling roles quickly and maintaining the quality of hires to support efficient operations.

As you juggle countless applications and work to fill open roles, it's normal to begin questioning your effectiveness as a recruiter. You might wonder if you're overlooking something or if there's a more efficient approach. These doubts can creep in and weigh heavily on you, making the process even more challenging. Now, let's turn to the impact self-doubt can have on recruitment.

Chapter 2:

The Weight of Self-Doubt—

Questioning Your Recruitment

Efficacy

You sit at your desk, staring at yet another rejection SMS message from a candidate you were sure would be the perfect fit. You start questioning yourself—did I ask the right questions? Did I miss any red flags? Was that awkward Zoom silence my fault? Self-doubt kicks in, and before you know it, you're spiraling. Maybe you're not cut out for recruitment after all. But deep down, you know that's not true. You've placed dozens of candidates successfully. So, why does one setback feel like the weight of the world?

And just when you're picking yourself up, another challenge hits—this time, it feels like a storm of never-ending tasks and obstacles.

Overwhelmed by Persistent Challenges

Recruiters in the service industry are often caught in a relentless cycle of stress and self-doubt, driven by unmanageable challenges like the constant rush to fill vacancies, frequent turnover, and adapting to ever-evolving technology. With each failed hire, delayed decision, and mounting pressure, recruiters face an emotional and professional toll that makes the job feel like an uphill battle.

Vicious Self-Enforcing Cycle

Recruiters in the service industry often find themselves caught in a relentless cycle of stress and burnout, fueled by high turnover rates, trainee setbacks, and constant technological shifts. With pressures mounting from all sides, even the most seasoned professionals can feel overwhelmed, questioning their ability to keep up in an ever-evolving field.

Pressure to Fill Vacancies Quickly

Recruiters in the service industry often face a continuous influx of challenges that raise stress levels and wear down even the most experienced professionals. As the obstacles keep coming—misaligned candidate expectations, sudden shifts in company needs, and unrealistic timelines—it's easy to feel like you're drowning in anxiety.

Each time a new hire doesn't pan out, the weight of those unresolved issues piles higher, leaving you overwhelmed and exhausted from the constant firefighting.

Continued High Trainee Failure Rate During Training

Dealing with frequent setbacks in trainee programs is one of the most difficult challenges. As a recruiter, you pour time and energy into identifying candidates you believe will succeed. You feel confident about your choices, only to be disappointed when trainees fail to meet expectations or drop out altogether.

It's not just a professional setback—it's personal. You vouched for these individuals who invested emotionally in their success. When they don't work out, it feels like a personal failure. You question your judgment and wonder if you're skilled at choosing suitable candidates. Over time, this cycle of failure can chip away at your confidence and add a heavy layer of frustration to your daily work.

Continued High Turnover Rate After Training

High turnover rates in the service industry exacerbate this problem. It's no secret that service jobs can be demanding, and many new hires burn out quickly, leading to a constant revolving door of employees. When staff leave, you're not just facing the challenge of finding replacements—you're doing it under pressure, knowing the organization depends on you to keep operations running smoothly. The urgency to fill the gap grows each time an employee exits, increasing your workload and stress.

As you scramble to meet hiring needs, it becomes harder to feel like you're making real progress, let alone achieve stability or accomplishment.

Constantly Changing Recruiting Technology and Strategies Requiring Recruiter Adaptation

The constant need to adapt recruitment strategies in response to changing trends, technologies, and industry demands only adds to the pressure. In theory, innovation sounds exciting but can be draining in practice. Between managing your regular tasks and staying on top of industry developments, the need to continually refine your strategies becomes exhausting. Sure, recruitment is a dynamic field that requires flexibility and creativity, but constantly being in "adaptation mode" can wear you down over time.

A 2023 study found that 53% of recruiters reported job burnout, with many citing the fast pace of recruitment as a significant contributor (*Recruiter Burnout*, n.d.). Burnout doesn't happen overnight; it creeps in when balancing adapting to changes and keeping up with day-to-day responsibilities becomes unsustainable. You start to feel the mental and emotional toll of constantly reinventing your approach, leaving you wondering whether you can keep up with the role's demands.

High Recruiter Burnout Rate

The intense demands of recruitment take an emotional and physical toll on professionals, often leading to burnout and self-doubt. Faced with high-pressure timelines, high turnover rates, and the constant challenge of finding suitable candidates, recruiters juggle multiple stressors with little time to reflect or recover.

Emotional Investment

The emotional investment that recruiters put into their work makes these challenges all the more taxing. Every candidate represents not just a potential employee but a person you've evaluated, invested in, and sometimes championed through the hiring process. When a hire turns out to be a bad fit, it's hard not to take it personally.

Recruiters often feel some level of personal responsibility when new hires fail. This emotional weight compounds with the practical difficulties, creating an environment where you're always one step behind, trying to fix problems that shouldn't have occurred in the first place.

Hiring Urgency

The constant pressure to fill open vacancies and ensure the new hires are a good fit for the team adds to the anxiety. The stakes feel higher when you know that a wrong hire could result in further turnover, setting you back even more. You might question decisions that typically felt simple and clear.

Long Time-To-Hire

Research by Glassdoor suggests that hiring a new employee in the US takes an average of 23.8 days (How Long Should Your Interview, 2017). For recruiters in the service industry, those days can feel like a race against time. There's pressure from hiring managers who need positions filled yesterday and candidates who may lose interest if the process drags on too long. Every delay, every misstep, adds more stress.

With so many variables at play, it's hard to feel you ultimately control the situation.

Compounding Stress

These factors combine to create an environment that makes it hard to catch your breath. The weight of continuous challenges, compounded by personal investment in the success of your hires, leads to an ongoing sense of stress. A study conducted by SHRM found that 65% of talent acquisition leaders report experiencing overwhelm, with many attributing it to the inundating demands of the job (Jendriks, 2023). It's a challenging role requiring resilience, adaptability, and a thick skin. But even the most seasoned recruiters are worn down by the unrelenting pressure.

And with all this emotional strain piling up, it's easy to wonder how much more you can handle, which brings us to the emotional toll that recruitment takes. You might not realize it at first, but this constant grind has a way of chipping away at your emotional well-being.

Recruitment Challenges' Toll on Recruiters' Well-Being

Professional challenges in recruitment extend far beyond daily tasks—they profoundly affect mental and physical well-being. The constant pressure to fill roles quickly, screen unqualified applicants, and meet company demands can lead to chronic stress, burnout, and even long-term health issues.

Not Just Burnout, But Also Impact on Mental Health

Professional challenges in recruitment take a significant toll on your well-being.

When you face persistent failures in finding suitable candidates, the weight of this burden doesn't just stay at work; it follows you home, affecting both your mental health and your personal life. Recruitment, especially in the service industry, is notoriously fast-paced and demanding. When a candidate falls through or doesn't live up to expectations, the disappointment builds up, often leading to anxiety, stress, or even depression.

A Sense of Guilt

One of the most significant contributors to this mental strain is the guilt you feel when you don't meet staffing needs.

You know how important your role is in keeping the business running smoothly. Without the right people in the correct positions, everything can fall apart. When things don't go as expected, you may feel like you've let the company down personally. This guilt can be overwhelming, leading to more profound self-doubt and inadequacy.

You start wondering if you're cut out for this job or even making the right decisions anymore.

Negatively Impact Personal Life

Professional stress extends beyond the workplace, impacting your personal life, relationships, and work–life balance. After a rough day, it's tough to leave that stress behind. You may be irritable or distracted with family and friends because work issues still occupy your mind. It's difficult to disconnect even when you're technically off the clock. Your job stays on your mind, making it hard to unwind or enjoy your downtime fully. This constant focus on work strains your relationships and makes you feel like you can never truly step away.

Recruitment in the service industry comes with heavy mental burdens, especially with its notoriously high turnover rates. In sectors like retail and hospitality, annual turnover can reach up to 60% (Eser, 2024a).

Impact on Physical Health

You may even notice that this stress leads to physical symptoms. Chronic stress can cause headaches, difficulty sleeping, and digestive issues, making it harder to function both at work and at home.

The National Institute for Occupational Safety and Health reports that prolonged exposure to work-related stress can cause serious health issues, such as cardiovascular disease (*About Stress*, 2024). In recruitment, the constant pressure to fill roles and meet company demands can quickly lead to burnout if not appropriately managed. Burnout, which the World Health Organization classifies as an "occupational phenomenon," is characterized by exhaustion, cynicism, and reduced professional efficacy (*Burn-Out*, 2019).

Once burnout sets in, recovering without a significant change in your work environment or lifestyle is difficult.

You might push through for a while, but the effects of unchecked stress are real and severe.

As you face these challenges, you might start questioning more than just your decisions. You may also begin to doubt the recruitment process itself.

Personal and Professional Reflection

It's that nagging thought creeping in at the end of a long day or, worse, during a meeting when you feel out of place—"Am I failing at my job?" This feeling isn't just uncomfortable; it can be debilitating, especially in a high-pressure role like recruitment. Self-doubt sneaks up and casts shadows on every decision, making even the most experienced recruiters question their abilities. You may have placed dozens of candidates successfully, yet one setback sends you into a spiral of second-guessing everything.

But here's the thing—self-doubt is indiscriminative. It's like a bad roommate who leaves dishes in the sink and turns every little hiccup into a catastrophe. You might start feeling it when a candidate ghosts you, a hiring manager questions your judgment, or metrics don't quite hit the mark. If left unchecked, this mindset can erode your confidence, making you less effective at your job. When uncertain, pitching a candidate convincingly, negotiating with authority, or building the relationships that lead to success is hard.

Understanding the Root Causes of Self-Doubt

But here's the truth—self-doubt is often more about perception than reality. Yes, it's natural to feel uncertainty, especially when the stakes are high, but if you zoom in on the data, you might find that the numbers aren't as bleak as your mind makes them out to be. For instance, if you miss a placement goal, consider the context: Were you managing more requisitions than usual? Did client requirements change mid-process? Are other recruiters facing similar issues?

Start by collecting data on your performance—objective, concrete facts. Track the number of successful placements, candidate feedback, and even interactions with hiring managers. Often, patterns emerge that show your "failures" are more about the recruiting systems you operate on than your capabilities. You're essentially managing an outdated recruiting system that produces poor results due to inefficiency.

This approach promotes healthy reflection. You're not ignoring problems; you're understanding them. When self-doubt creeps in, look at the numbers, the patterns, and the external factors that might be at play. You realize the real problem lies in the recruiting strategy and system.

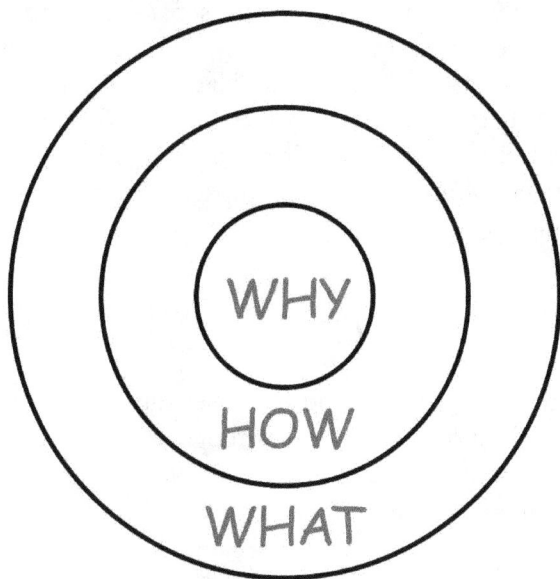

Seeking Answers to Persistent Problems

So, how do you move from a place of debilitating doubt to one of purposeful action? Shifting the narrative from "What am I doing wrong?" to "What's going on here? How and why?" (See image above.) You're not just second-guessing yourself; you're seeking to understand the more profound, systemic issues that might impact your results. This type of reflection is where real growth happens—not just for you as a recruiter but for the entire recruitment process.

Set the Stage for Exploring Deeper Systemic Issues in Recruitment

Let's say you're struggling to fill a position open for months. At first, you might think, "I'm not finding the right talent." But if you dig deeper, you might discover the job description is vague, the compensation isn't competitive, or the hiring manager keeps changing requirements. In cases like these, self-doubt makes you feel like you're missing the mark, but the reality is that no amount of sourcing wizardry can fix a broken process.

Taking a step back and analyzing the larger picture separates personal performance from systemic problems. This way, you're not just tackling the symptoms—missing placements, candidate drop-offs—but addressing the root issues that create these problems in the first place. When you shift your mindset to explore what's driving your challenges, you better understand where you can make an impact and where you need to advocate for change within your organization.

From Self-Doubt to Self-Discovery

Ultimately, shifting from a self-doubt mindset to self-discovery isn't just about feeling better—it's about becoming a stronger, more resilient recruiter. Self-doubt will always appear, especially in a field as dynamic as recruitment. But you can learn to use it as a signal, not a verdict.

When that voice in your head starts to say, *Am I failing at my job?* answer back with facts, data, and a willingness to dig deeper. What's going on? What external factors are at play? Where can you focus your energy to make a real difference? By transforming self-doubt into a springboard for reflection and action, you boost your confidence and create a healthier, more effective recruitment process.

So, are you failing at your job? Probably not. You're just asking the wrong question. Instead, ask yourself, *What can I learn from this?* Then, use that insight to fuel your growth and rethink the more profound issues: your recruiting strategy and recruiting system.

Key Takeaways

- Recruiters in the service industry face persistent stress and self-doubt due to high turnover rates, time pressures, and evolving recruitment demands.

- Emotional investment in candidates and setbacks, such as high trainee failure rates, contribute to burnout, which impacts professional confidence and personal life.

- Constantly adapting to changing recruitment technologies and strategies adds to the exhaustion, often making recruiters feel inadequate despite their achievements.

- External factors and system inefficiencies magnify self-doubt, making recruiters question their abilities rather than recognize structural issues.

- Shifting from self-doubt to purposeful self-reflection enables recruiters to identify and address systemic problems, strengthening personal resilience and the recruitment process.

As you navigate self-doubt and persistent challenges, another issue lurks beneath the surface—the overwhelming flood of unqualified applicants. It's like an iceberg you didn't see coming, and it complicates everything. Let's look closer at how this hidden problem disrupts your recruitment process in the next chapter.

Chapter 3:

Unveiling the Hidden Iceberg—

The Unqualified Applicant Flood

You're a recruiter, sipping your third coffee of the morning, bracing yourself to screen 200 resumes. By application #50, you're knee-deep in irrelevant work histories and wild career leaps. Barista applying for a management role? Sure, why not? You even spot a "professional clown" vying for a senior HR position. You rub your eyes, wondering how long before the real candidates surface.

It's not that people aren't applying; too many shouldn't be.

That's the hidden iceberg recruiters face. Let's move on to the next topic: too many unqualified applicants.

The Surface Problem: Too Many Unqualified Applicants

Recruitment teams in the service industry frequently face a severe issue: an overwhelming number of unqualified applicants for open positions. This issue significantly disrupts productivity and hampers operational efficiency. Imagine needing to hire a front-line service worker quickly. Still, instead of suitable candidates, you're swamped with hundreds of unqualified applicants.

This scenario goes beyond frustration; it's a massive drain on time and resources, especially when quality hires are vital to maintaining service standards.

The Disconnect Between Quantity and Quality

While it might seem beneficial to have many applications, the reality is often the opposite. When most candidates don't meet basic requirements, the misalignment between quantity and quality becomes a glaring issue. This is particularly problematic in industries like hospitality and retail, where filling positions rapidly is essential. An overflow of unqualified applicants can significantly slow down the entire recruitment process, causing a ripple effect on operational performance.

TeamStage reported hospitality recruiters and found that they receive an average of 250 applications for each job posting. Still, only 25% of the applicants meet the minimum qualifications (*Job Interview Statistics*, n.d.).

Delays can cause you to miss opportunities in fast-paced environments where skilled employees are in high demand. For instance, a hotel might urgently need a new front-desk supervisor. If the job posting attracts a high volume of underqualified applicants, the hiring manager could easily overlook a strong candidate simply because the process took too long.

The Time and Resource Drain on Recruiters

The time spent sifting through unqualified applications is one of the most significant issues recruiters face. Spending most of their day screening irrelevant candidates detracts from engaging with high-potential talent that could benefit the company. Industries like retail and hospitality, known for high turnover and constant hiring needs, are hit hardest by this problem.

According to recent data, the applicant-to-interview ratio in 2023 was just 2% (Farris, 2024). Of every 100 applicants, only 2 received an interview invitation. A low ratio shows that many applicants either don't meet the qualifications or become disengaged during the hiring process, leading to interview ghosting.

This inefficiency can slow down the hiring process, making it harder for companies to swiftly attract and secure top talent. When the process drags on, it frustrates recruiters and leaves a negative impression on jobseekers, who may accept offers from more responsive employers.

Burnout and Reduced Job Satisfaction

Recruiters often describe the burnout of combing through hundreds of irrelevant applications to find a handful of qualified candidates. For example, a fast-food chain might receive over 300 applications for a single cashier position. Still, if 75% of those candidates lack the required customer service experience, that's a lot of wasted time. The stress from this kind of workload can lead to decreased job satisfaction among recruiters, ultimately impacting their performance and well-being.

This overload doesn't just affect the recruiters—it can damage the company's reputation. Suppose the hiring process becomes too slow or disorganized. In that case, candidates may vent their frustrations on platforms like Glassdoor, potentially turning away future talent. According to a CareerArc study, 72% of service industry job seekers who had a negative hiring experience said they would share their stories on social media, further hurting the company's ability to attract quality candidates in the future (*2022 Guide to Candidate Experience*, 2021).

Now that we've discussed the visible symptoms of a broken recruitment process—namely, the influx of unqualified applicants—it's essential to understand what drives these issues. The next topic will address the underlying causes of this problem, including unclear job descriptions, lack of alignment between hiring goals and strategies, and inadequate screening methods. Understanding these hidden factors will provide deeper insight into why the problem persists, setting the stage for a more practical approach.

Real Hidden Causes

Suppose you're finding that your service industry business regularly receives applications from underqualified candidates. In that case, it's time to dig deeper and identify the hidden factors contributing to this trend. It's not always about applicant skills; sometimes, how the marketplace perceives your company is the root cause. The critical hidden issue is the failure to attract qualified applicants—or, more precisely, applicants with the right fit. Therefore, you need to focus on attracting suitable candidates to decrease the number of unqualified applicants.

Assessing Company Appeal: Who Will Be Attracted to You?

Start by evaluating if your organization is considered an attractive workplace. Company appeal isn't just about paychecks—it's about how job seekers perceive your brand, values, benefits, and growth opportunities. Companies with solid reputations attract many candidates. Still, not all of them suit the offered roles. A well-perceived brand can discourage unqualified applicants (I am not good enough for this company) *and* attract higher-quality candidates.

Evaluating Compensation and Benefits: The Higher, the More Qualified

Your compensation package can either attract top-tier talent or less-qualified applicants, depending on how it compares to industry standards. Service industry employees consider compensation their top priority when evaluating job offers. It's not just about base salary—bonuses, health insurance, retirement savings, and other perks matter, too.

For instance, Hilton saw a surge in qualified applicants when it launched the "Go Hilton Team Member" travel program, which offered discounted stays for employees and their families (Fuentes, 2023). This program didn't just attract more candidates—it brought in experienced professionals who valued the work–life balance and the company's focus on employee satisfaction. If your compensation is below industry standards, you may attract those looking for temporary work rather than building a career in your company.

Company Values and Culture: Attract the Like-Minded

What your organization stands for can significantly impact candidate quality. A strong company culture doesn't just engage current employees; it also attracts like-minded candidates who are more likely to be qualified. Service industry businesses with well-defined cultures experience higher employee engagement, translating into better applicant quality.

For example, Chick-fil-A's commitment to service excellence and employee respect means that jobseekers who value those attributes are more likely to apply (Wells, 2024). This approach draws in candidates who possess the right skills and align with the company's values. In contrast, companies with unclear or misaligned values may see an influx of candidates who don't resonate with the company's culture, even if they meet the technical qualifications.

Opportunities for Growth and Development: Define Long-Term or a Stop-Gap Job

Potential employees often scrutinize the development opportunities a company offers before applying. A lack of clear career paths can attract candidates who see the job as a short-term stop-gap rather than a strategic career move. In the service industry, workers are likelier to stay with companies that provide career advancement options.

Consider The Cheesecake Factory, known for its robust management training programs (Ruiz, 2006). This emphasis on professional development attracts ambitious professionals looking to build a long-term career in hospitality rather than those seeking temporary employment. Without offering these opportunities, your company may attract candidates who view it as a temporary stop in their career path.

Genuine Care for Employees: Applicant Can See It Miles Away

Prioritizing employee well-being has become essential for a company's attractiveness. Organizations with solid wellness initiatives experience lower turnover rates and higher levels of job satisfaction. Hyatt, for instance, has become known for its Hyatt Thrive program, which focuses on employee well-being, physical health, and emotional support (*Hyatt Announces Hyatt Thrive*, 2011). This commitment helps attract motivated, experienced applicants rather than those looking for a quick paycheck.

If your company needs to prioritize employee well-being visibly, it could attract candidates who prioritize job security over job satisfaction, which might be better for low-engagement roles.

Company Reputation and Social Responsibility: Show Kindness and Attract Kindhearted Applicants

Your organization's reputation can boost or obstruct your recruitment efforts. Companies known for ethical practices, employee satisfaction, and strong community involvement generally receive more applications from well-qualified candidates. Businesses with a positive reputation experience reduced hiring costs and received more applications from high-quality candidates.

For example, Starbucks is renowned for its commitment to employee development and community service, making it a top choice for candidates who value corporate responsibility. Conversely, suppose your company has a damaged reputation or poor employee reviews. In that case, you'll likely have difficulty attracting top-tier talent. You may hire candidates unaware of these issues or have limited employment opportunities. The visible issue of too many unqualified applicants and its hidden causes are summarized in the illustration below.

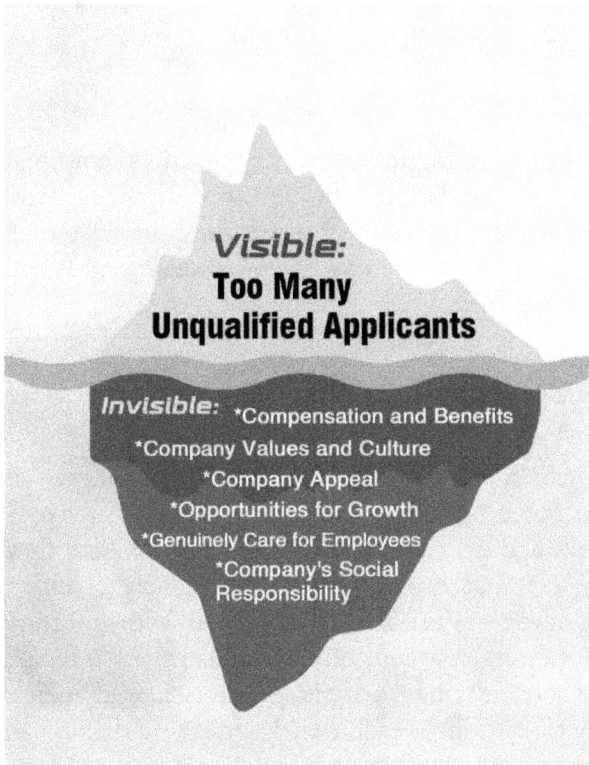

Visible:
Too Many
Unqualified Applicants

Invisible: *Compensation and Benefits
*Company Values and Culture
*Company Appeal
*Opportunities for Growth
*Genuinely Care for Employees
*Company's Social
Responsibility

When a company's appeal attracts a disproportionate number of unqualified candidates, it can disrupt the entire recruitment process. The next topic will focus on this phenomenon's impact on recruitment efficiency, time-to-fill metrics, and overall hiring strategies, specifically within the service industry. Addressing these issues is crucial for refining your talent acquisition strategy and ensuring you build a robust, capable workforce.

The Impact on Recruitment

Attracting the wrong candidates can seem like a minor setback, but it carries consequences that ripple through every part of an organization. From deterring top talent to overloading your current team, poor hires can undermine productivity, profitability, and long-term success.

Attracting the Wrong Candidates: It Is Even Worse Than What It Appears

When struggling to fill a role, settling for just any applicant is tempting. However, hiring the wrong candidate can be far more damaging than initially seems. The impact goes beyond just a mismatch in skills or a lack of experience—it can negatively influence your team, repel top talent, and undermine your company's long-term success.

Turning Away the Right Talent

Attracting the wrong candidates doesn't just waste your time—it actively turns away the qualified talent you want. Think of it like a crowded store: When unqualified candidates flood your pipeline, they create noise and confusion that drowns out the genuinely qualified ones. Most top talent doesn't want to be associated with a hiring process that seems chaotic or filled with unfit candidates. As a result, they'll often look elsewhere, leaving you with a pool skewed in the wrong direction. It's a vicious cycle—each poorly fitting candidate can push another strong one away, making finding the talent you need even harder.

Undermining Your Existing Team

Bad hires don't just affect your candidate pool—they also impact your current employees. One of the main reasons talented employees decide to leave is dealing with coworkers who fail to contribute their fair share. Imagine how frustrating it is for your best performers to work twice as hard because their colleagues can't meet basic expectations. Coworker frustration is a primary turnover driver, especially in high-stress industries like hospitality. When unqualified hires join the team, your strong performers have to pick up the slack, leading to burnout and resentment.

In the long run, this means losing the very people who make your company great, all because they're tired of working alongside unqualified or poorly aligned teammates. So, while it may seem like adding an extra body to the team solves a problem, it could set you up for an even bigger issue—one that could see your top talent walking out the door.

Eroding Long-Term Performance and Profitability

There's also a broader, long-term impact. Unqualified hires don't just underperform—they can drag down the entire organization's productivity and profitability. When team members consistently miss targets or don't fit into the company culture, overall performance takes a hit. Over time, this degrades your company's reputation, impacts customer satisfaction, and reduces profitability.

It's not just about the present. These mistakes can have a lasting impact, damaging your ability to attract and keep talented employees. Hiring the wrong people can foster a culture of mediocrity that's incredibly difficult to break free from. This isn't merely a temporary problem; it's a long-term threat to your company's success.

Increasing the Workload for Everyone Involved

Finally, let's talk about the day-to-day headaches. Managing a poor hire can significantly impact your managers, recruiters, and HR team. You spend more time on performance reviews, disciplinary actions, and rehiring—creating a constant firefighting cycle. Every unqualified candidate who makes it through wastes time during the hiring process and drains resources long after the ink drains on the contract.

The increased workload creates a bottleneck, slowly bringing on the right talent and draining energy that the team could use elsewhere. Before you know it, the cost of a bad hire isn't just about dollars and cents—it's about lost time, increased stress, and a constant feeling of being one step behind.

Attracting the wrong candidates affects your ability to attract top talent, strains your current team, reduces profitability, and adds to everyone's workload. When it comes to recruitment, aim for excellence. Don't get trapped in a compromise. Focusing on finding the right fit isn't just about filling a role—it's about safeguarding the health and success of your entire organization.

Rethinking Your Recruiting Strategy

We must reevaluate our job design, sourcing strategies, brand positioning, screening methods, and engagement processes to reduce the large influx of unqualified applicants. The high volume of unqualified candidates is just the beginning of a deeper issue. You'll learn more about screening and advocacy in Chapter 11.

Key Takeaways

- Recruiters in the service industry face an influx of unqualified applicants, which significantly strains productivity and hampers efficient hiring processes.

- This imbalance between the quantity and quality of applicants leads to delays, with only 25% of candidates meeting minimum qualifications, as reported in the hospitality sector.

- Unqualified applications waste recruiters' time, contributing to burnout and reduced job satisfaction, and detract from meaningful engagement with high-potential talent.

- Attracting underqualified candidates affects the existing workforce by increasing turnover and decreasing productivity, leading to long-term profitability challenges.

- Rethinking recruitment strategies, including job design, sourcing, and screening, is essential to reducing the number of unqualified applicants and protecting organizational success.

While addressing the hidden iceberg of the high number of unqualified applicants is vital, another challenge awaits: competitors attracting your top candidates with better offers. In the fast-paced service industry, skilled professionals often have multiple options. Understanding how to prevent losing them to more enticing opportunities is crucial. Let's dive into how competitors beyond the obvious can sway your best talent.

Chapter 4:

Competitors Beyond the Obvious—Losing Candidates to Better Offers

You've got the perfect candidate lined up—everything's moving smoothly. Then, boom! You get the dreaded email: "I've accepted another offer." A competitor you hadn't considered ended up winning them over. Maybe it's a company with deeper pockets, a flashier brand, or one that offers unlimited snack breaks (seriously, who can compete with that?). The point is, you're left scratching your head, wondering where you lost your edge. It's like getting ghosted after a promising first date—frustrating and confusing.

The real issue usually has nothing to do with the snacks.

Sometimes, what looks like a better job on paper is more about perception than reality. Why do candidates leave for what appear to be better opportunities? Let's take a closer look.

The Surface Issue: Candidates Choosing "Better" Jobs

It's incredibly frustrating when you've invested time and effort in a candidate, only to lose them to a seemingly "better" offer at the final stages. But this happens more often in today's competitive job market than recruiters would like. CareerPlug reports that 58% of candidates rejected job offers because of poor experience. In comparison, 80% said a positive experience strongly influenced their decision to accept the offer (*2021 Candidate Experience Report*, 2022). So, what's going wrong?

The Frustration of Declined Offers

One of the most disheartening moments for recruiters is when top candidates turn down an offer.

This situation happens more often than you might expect. According to a 2019 study, 28% of candidates have accepted a job offer only to back out before their start date, often due to better offers, second thoughts about the role, or even a sudden change in personal circumstances (Half, 2019). Such last-minute decisions don't just feel like a punch in the gut—they derail timelines, disrupt project planning, and create added stress for teams already stretched thin, impacting morale and leading to burnout. You magnify the loss when you consider its ripple effect on the business. Suddenly, the team is back at square one, scrambling to restart the hiring process and reevaluate other candidates while ensuring that business goals and deadlines don't suffer.

Wasted Time and Resources

When candidates drop out late in the hiring process, it's more than a disappointment—it represents a substantial loss of time, energy, and resources. Recruiters meticulously plan and coordinate every step of the hiring process, from writing job posts and reviewing resumes to scheduling interviews and completing background checks. When a candidate exits unexpectedly, all the effort put into getting them through each stage ends up being for nothing, causing frustration and tangible setbacks.

For companies, a delayed hiring decision doesn't just prolong the search; it can also inflate hiring costs and impact the current team's morale. When a role remains unfilled, other team members often have to step in and take on additional responsibilities. This increases their workload, leading to potential burnout and decreased overall productivity. What might have started as a promising candidate experience can quickly turn sour if they're left waiting without clear updates, fueling negative perceptions about the company. You'll learn more about screening and advocacy in Chapter 11.

A Silver Lining: Potentially Overqualified Applicant

One silver lining when a candidate accepts a better offer is realizing they might have been overqualified for the role, making them less ideal for the position. Why consider this a silver lining? Hiring an overqualified applicant would actually be a worse outcome for both the recruiter and the company.

Interestingly, hiring overqualified candidates can be a double-edged sword. On one hand, they can bring valuable experience and fresh perspectives to a role, driving productivity and innovation. On the other hand, they may leave quickly if their pay and job experience expectations don't align with reality.

While overqualified employees can initially contribute to your organization's success, mismatched expectations can lead to turnover. Setting expectations during the interview process is crucial, as well as ensuring that the candidate understands the potential challenges and opportunities. Moreover, it is a recruiter's duty to ensure that candidates conduct their due diligence.

While declined offers and resource waste are apparent pain points, we must discover their hidden causes. Let's investigate these hidden causes to understand what's driving qualified talent away.

Real Hidden Causes

Securing top talent in today's market means recognizing that competition extends beyond industry lines, and many factors influence a candidate's decision. By identifying hidden challenges like indirect competition, job design, and candidate experience, you can refine your recruitment strategy and position your company as the ideal choice for skilled professionals.

The Probability Game: Play It to Win

Recruiting runs on probabilities, so as a recruiter, you need to anticipate that candidates will not accept a certain percentage of offers, and be mentally and practically ready for this likelihood.

Preparing for this means ensuring enough volume. For instance, with a 50% chance of offer declines, hiring 2 trainees requires extending 4 offers—not fewer.

However, the real issue isn't just playing the probability game—it's the level you're playing. Does your recruiting process see 50% of offers declined, or is it closer to 20%? This distinction is essential. Your goal should be to play the probability game at the more favorable level—in this case, 20%.

Overlooking Indirect Competitors

It's easy to assume that your competitors are limited to companies within the same industry. Still, this narrow viewpoint can lead to missed opportunities and unexpected challenges when securing top talent. Many organizations fail to realize that indirect competitors from different sectors are vying for the same skilled candidates. This oversight can result in losing talent to companies you hadn't considered a threat.

For instance, a financial services firm searching for data analysts might suddenly struggle to attract candidates because tech startups or ecommerce giants offer higher salaries and attractive benefits like remote work options and flexible schedules.

Looking beyond direct rivals makes it possible to understand the broader market dynamics better. For instance, companies that once primarily recruited customer service representatives now compete against tech firms seeking similar interpersonal skills for roles like user experience and customer success. These shifts show how indirect competitors can emerge rapidly, disrupting traditional recruitment strategies and making it even harder to secure top talent.

Staying agile is as crucial as skill sets, once limited to specific industries like technology and finance, now apply to a wider range of market opportunities.

Job Design

Compensation alone no longer persuades top talent to accept an offer.

Comprehensive benefits packages have become equally essential to making a job offer attractive. A SHRM study found that 66% of young workers prioritize benefits like health insurance and professional development programs when considering job offers (Rockwood, 2022).

Today's most competitive offers provide a clear path for growth and an environment where employees feel genuinely valued.

Promoting Job Strengths Based on Applicant Needs

Enhance your job's appeal by aligning it with targeted applicants' needs and goals.

Understanding what motivates candidates is crucial in shaping a compelling job offer. Career advancement is critical for some, while others prioritize work–life balance, flexibility, daytime hours, or a positive company culture. The pandemic prompted many workers to reassess their priorities, increasing the value placed on personal growth, meaningful work, and a sense of purpose.

By understanding these diverse motivations, you can position your company as a preferred choice and craft offers that align with candidates' needs.

Effectively communicating your job's strengths at each stage of the recruitment process is essential. The more your job meets an applicant's needs, the less likely they'll accept another offer.

Achieving this requires well-designed roles and skillful promotion of job benefits.

A Silver Lining: An Applicant Might Be Overqualified

Sometimes, losing candidates to other industries isn't necessarily a negative outcome—it could signal that your applicants might have more potential than you initially realized. Recognizing when a candidate is overqualified allows you to pivot your approach, offering roles that better align with their career aspirations.

While losing candidates to better offers might seem like the apparent reason for recruitment challenges, the reality is often more nuanced. What if it's not just about salary or perks? Sometimes, the root cause lies more profoundly in company culture, job design, candidate experience, or even subtle gaps in your employer branding.

Key Takeaways

- Candidates frequently leave for more appealing jobs, though these opportunities often don't meet expectations. This can result in a cycle of job-hopping, where candidates switch roles without fully understanding the drawbacks of each new position.

- Declined offers happen regularly as candidates weigh factors like previous job experiences and last-minute competitor offers. Even a tiny shift in perception can influence their decision, making it crucial to address these variables early on.

- When candidates back out late in hiring, you lose valuable time and resources. It affects team morale, as everyone must adjust to the ongoing vacancy. This disruption can set back projects and create additional strain on current employees.

- Recruitment faces competition from other industries that now seek similar skill sets, making it harder to retain candidates drawn to different fields. Nontraditional sectors may offer attractive incentives, widening the range of options and drawing talent away from service roles.

- Designing job roles thoughtfully and highlighting benefits that candidates genuinely value can help reduce last-minute offer rejections. When you tailor offers to meet candidates' needs from the start, they're more likely to commit, lowering the risk of a declined offer.

You've secured the perfect hire, overcoming fierce competition and last-minute surprises. The real challenge now is ensuring new talent thrives in training. Ironically, what will happen in training has been primarily determined by what has already happened—the quality of your recruiting.

Chapter 5:

The Training Paradox—When

Recruitment Sabotages

Development

Imagine this: You hire a fresh-faced recruit, excited to join the team, only to see their enthusiasm nosedive after just a few weeks. They get a "training manual" that reads like a corporate version of *War and Peace*. By the time the onboarding process ends, they lose interest and motivation. They failed to meet the standard of training success. So, what happened? Has the training program been unable to do the job?

Now, let's look at ineffective training programs that turn potential into missed opportunities.

The Apparent Problem: Ineffective Training Programs

When new trainees struggle to perform, it's easy to blame training programs. However, the real issue often lies more profoundly in ineffective hiring practices that fail to align new hires with company culture and role requirements. Without addressing these underlying problems, training alone can't bridge the gap.

Blaming Training for High Failure Rates

When employees don't meet expectations, companies often scrutinize their training programs as the primary culprit. Training is a high-visibility component of employee development and an easy target when performance falters. However, focusing solely on training might miss the real issue. Research shows that 89% of new hires fail due to poor attitudes, lack of motivation, or a mismatch with the company culture rather than lacking technical skills (*Beware of Candidates*, n.d.). This statistic suggests that the underlying problem frequently begins well before training even enters the picture.

Companies might offer comprehensive sales training on product knowledge, sales techniques, and negotiation strategies. However, if new hires don't align with the company's culture or approach to building customer relationships, this training is unlikely to yield the desired results. Sales professionals might possess the right technical skills but fail to succeed because they don't resonate with the company's values or customer engagement strategies.

The customer service industry offers another example. Many organizations implement extensive onboarding programs to equip representatives with the skills to handle various inquiries, complaints, and scenarios. The training covers everything from using the company's software to managing challenging customer interactions. But even a perfectly executed training program can't compensate for a lack of empathy, patience, or a genuine commitment to helping customers. If recruiters overlook these attributes during the hiring process, it can lead to mismatches and future performance issues. In that case, the training is unlikely to transform an indifferent new hire into a passionate advocate for the brand.

These scenarios illustrate that poor performance post-training is often less about the training program itself and more about the initial hiring decisions. Companies frequently fail to consider whether a candidate's values align with the organization's mission or if they possess the nontechnical attributes that are just as crucial for success. This approach often sets new hires up for failure from the outset, even after they complete the training program.

Costs Associated With Training Failures

Training failures often lead to significant expenses, and when organizations misattribute these failures to flawed training programs, the overall costs can quickly escalate.

In 2016 alone, U.S. companies invested over $70 billion in training initiatives, with large organizations shelling out as much as $13 million each (Freifeld, 2016). Despite such significant spending, the reality is stark: Almost 90% of new skills acquired through training sessions are forgotten within a year if not consistently reinforced (*Forgetting Curve*, n.d.).

This statistic reveals more than wasted dollars—it showcases a missed opportunity that can lead to lower productivity and employee morale.

The repercussions extend far beyond initial training costs. Employees who feel unprepared or unsupported due to inadequate training or misalignment with their roles tend to become disengaged. In service industries, such disengagement is palpable. For example, when a hotel receptionist feels disengaged, they may handle guest complaints poorly, resulting in negative reviews and a decline in brand loyalty. As disengagement grows, turnover rates rise—a familiar yet costly problem.

High turnover doesn't just mean repeating the same training expenses. It also entails losing valuable time and productivity, especially in roles requiring soft skills, like restaurant managers or customer service agents, where a deep understanding of the business is crucial. When a trained employee departs, the company has to go through the entire recruitment and training cycle again, resulting in a loss of momentum and increased expenses.

Blaming training programs for performance failures might seem logical when employees underperform or struggle to meet expectations. However, the root of the problem is often deeper, lying in recruitment and role alignment.

In a fast-paced restaurant setting, for example, hiring someone who thrives in a structured environment but struggles with multitasking will lead to poor performance, no matter how comprehensive the training program is. The same goes for hiring a customer service representative who lacks empathy or resilience—traits complex to instill through training alone.

Ultimately, the cycle of training, turnover, and morale issues results in an expensive treadmill that keeps the organization stuck, draining resources and lowering efficiency without ever addressing the underlying problems.

Real Hidden Cause: Faulty Recruitment

The recruitment process is often the overlooked culprit behind training challenges and high turnover rates. Rushing to fill roles can lead to hiring candidates with skill gaps or misaligned values, disrupting team dynamics and impacting customer experience. To solve this, organizations must prioritize thorough candidate evaluations and align hiring criteria with future training demands.

Ignoring Red Flags During Hiring

Hiring the right candidate is crucial for immediate role success and long-term organizational growth.

However, many organizations rush the recruitment process, often ignoring early warning signs that could signal a poor fit. These red flags might include unexplained gaps in employment history, inconsistent job performance, or behavior that doesn't align with the company's values and culture.

For example, hiring a restaurant server who has switched jobs frequently without clear reasons in the service industry could indicate an inability to commit or resolve workplace challenges. Dismissing these early indicators results in onboarding candidates who are not just mismatched for the job but also lack the foundational skills to succeed in training or development programs.

The pressure to fill positions quickly can push recruiters to focus solely on surface-level qualifications like educational background, previous titles, or short-term experience without delving deeper into the candidate's adaptability, emotional intelligence (EQ), or learning potential. This scenario is widespread in high-turnover industries such as retail or hospitality, where managers might feel compelled to hire a candidate who "looks good on paper" simply to keep operations running. However, this can lead to significant issues down the road.

For example, a retail store might hire a candidate with years of experience in a similar role but fail to assess whether they can handle that store's high-pressure, customer-centric nature. This candidate may look ideal initially, yet struggle to navigate conflicts or manage peak hours, disrupting the team dynamic and leading to further turnover. Similarly, in a hotel setting, hiring someone who has a polished resume but lacks the interpersonal skills necessary for handling demanding guests can result in a poor customer experience, ultimately impacting the business's reputation.

The emphasis on quickly filling roles can overshadow a thorough evaluation of qualities like collaboration, flexibility, and problem-solving. Such oversights often come to light during training programs, where a candidate who seemed promising on paper struggles to grasp core concepts or adapt to the organization's specific requirements. As a result, the initial effort to save time in the hiring process can cost far more in resources, morale, and missed growth opportunities.

Great Hires Even Train Themselves!

Training won't fix a poor hiring choice, even with extra investment; on the flip side, an excellent hire will often self-train, driven by the motivation to succeed in the role.

What a difference it makes.

Many organizations still frequently overlook the connection between recruitment and training. Still, it can significantly impact overall business success, especially in retail or hospitality industries where customer experience is paramount. Selecting the wrong candidate can cause a ripple effect of training challenges, disrupting individual development and the entire team's efficiency. For instance, hiring a new restaurant staff member without verifying their ability to handle high-pressure environments may result in a chaotic training period. Such mismatches often leave the new hire and existing team members struggling to adapt, leading to prolonged onboarding times and increased frustration. Hence, the real root cause is poor recruiting.

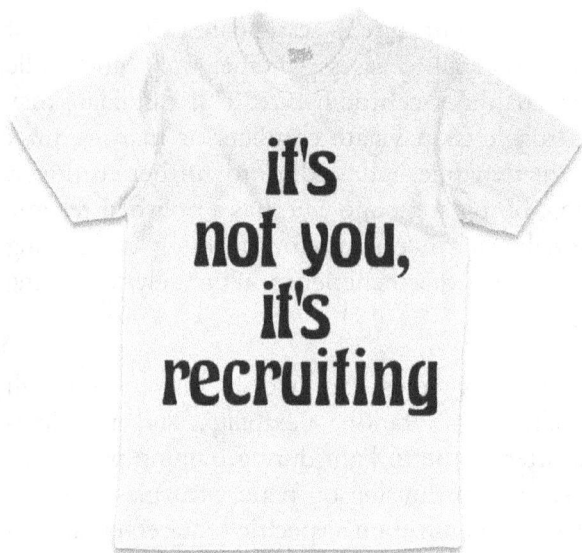

The Necessity of Recruitment Overhaul

Recruiting suitable candidates demands a strategic overhaul rooted in data-driven insights and long-term alignment with training objectives. By integrating structured hiring methods and leveraging technology, you ensure that each process step is intentional, objective, and aligned with the organization's goals.

Hire Better With Data Insights

To choose the best candidates, you need to set up a solid data structure that supports the effective use of insights. This means reworking your recruitment process to capture the correct data, analyze it accurately, and make informed decisions based on your findings. You build a talent pipeline that lets you confidently identify and select candidates, with each step supported by clear evidence rather than relying on gut feelings.

Selective hiring involves structured interviews, realistic job previews, and assessment tools like work tests to evaluate ability, trainability, and commitment. For example, structured interviews predict a candidate's future job performance more than unstructured ones, making them a key component in aligning hiring with training goals.

Aligning Recruitment With Training Objectives

To effectively bridge recruitment and training, ensure your hiring strategy aligns with your organization's long-term development goals. One of the company's most significant mistakes is separating these two processes, resulting in mismatches that ultimately undermine employees' success. Integrating recruitment and training starts with a collaborative approach: HR and training departments should work closely to define success and then use those definitions to refine recruitment criteria.

Utilizing Technology to Bridge the Gap

Modern technology can bridge recruitment and training by providing data-driven insights into candidate potential and training readiness. Recruiters can use applicant tracking systems (ATS) to incorporate training data, making it easier to evaluate whether a candidate's abilities align with the expected training results. Additionally, companies can use shared platforms to track the progress of training efforts and refine recruitment strategies based on performance data.

Finally, companies can use AI technology to interview candidates more consistently and objectively. You can deploy AI prediction models to improve hiring efficiency, which reduces time-to-hire, turnover rates, and recruitment costs. You can learn more about how AI technology can be helpful in recruitment in Chapter 14.

Companies using technology to integrate these processes can increase the success rate of new hires. This shows the powerful impact that a tech-enabled approach can have on aligning hiring and training.

Creating a Continuous Feedback Loop

A critical component of this integration is establishing a continuous feedback loop between recruiting and training teams. Regular communication allows both teams to refine their strategies based on real-world outcomes. For example, suppose trainers notice that new hires need help with a specific aspect of training. In that case, they can relay this feedback to recruiters, who can adjust their selection criteria to focus on candidates with more vital foundational skills. According to a study by the Center for American Progress, turnover can cost an organization anywhere from 16% to 213% of an employee's salary, making it essential to address these issues early on (Eser, 2024a).

Training failures often occur because of factors outside the training program itself. Instead, poor recruiting is the real culprit. It's about hiring the right talent to support growth, enhance performance, and, ultimately, contribute to the organization's long-term success.

Key Takeaways

- Ineffective training programs often mask deeper issues in hiring practices that overlook candidate alignment with company culture and role requirements.

- Many new hires fail due to mismatched attitudes or values rather than lacking technical skills, highlighting the importance of cultural fit during recruitment.

- High turnover and disengagement, particularly in customer-facing roles, can often be traced back to hiring decisions that neglected essential soft skills.

- Structured recruitment strategies, like data-driven insights and technology tools, help align hiring with training outcomes and ensure long-term success.

- A feedback loop between recruitment and training teams allows ongoing adjustments to recruitment criteria, reducing turnover and improving overall performance.

Recruiting and aligning suitable candidates with training objectives is only part of the battle. The next challenge is navigating through overwhelming applicant volumes without sacrificing quality. When your time-to-hire slows down, it's not just efficiency that suffers—it can also impact candidate experience and overall morale.

Chapter 6:

The Time-To-Hire Dilemma—

Swamped by Applicant Volume

Imagine this: You post a job opening, grab your coffee, and return to find your inbox exploding with 200 applications. It's like planning a small BBQ and ending up with the whole neighborhood showing up. You start sorting through resumes, but after the tenth "passionate team player," your eyes glaze over, and you wonder if you'll ever see the bottom of the pile. At this rate, you'll need an assistant to hire an assistant! Sound familiar?

The real problem is that this volume bottleneck often leads to painfully prolonged hiring timelines, which brings us to the next issue: Prolonged hiring lead time.

The Surface Issue: Prolonged Hiring Timelines

If you've ever felt the pain of an open position lingering on your to-do list for weeks—or even months—you're not alone. Slow hiring timelines are more than just a minor inconvenience; they can snowball into more significant issues for your organization. From struggling to sift through a mountain of applications to scheduling interviews with busy managers, each process phase seems to hit one snag after another.

The result? Bottlenecks that frustrate candidates and overburden your team. However, the surface issue often exceeds just a lack of efficiency.

Inability to Process Applicants Quickly

When applications start flooding in, the initial excitement of a busy hiring season can quickly give way to dread.

In the service industry—where customer-facing roles like servers, front-desk staff, and customer support agents are crucial—recruitment teams often find themselves overwhelmed by sheer volume. Picture a popular restaurant chain receiving 500 resumes for a single position. With so many to sort through, identifying top talent becomes daunting, leading to prolonged screening phases and a painfully slow hiring timeline.

Losing Top Candidates Due to Delays

The repercussions of slow hiring aren't just internal. Top candidates in the service industry, particularly those with specialized skills or extensive experience, tend to have multiple job offers. Research from Robert Half (2016) shows that 39% of candidates expect a decision within 7–14 days. When hiring takes too long, top candidates often lose interest and pursue other opportunities. Imagine a skilled barista or an experienced concierge waiting weeks without feedback—they're more likely to accept a competitor's offer, leaving you scrambling to fill the gap.

One real-world example is a midsized hotel chain that posted openings for front-desk managers. Due to a high volume of applications and a lack of automated screening tools, it took HR three weeks to shortlist candidates for initial interviews. By the time they reached out to the top applicants, two had already accepted positions elsewhere. This "time kills all deals" effect is a recruiter's nightmare—losing candidates they worked hard to source because the timeline didn't align.

Operational Inefficiencies and Resource Drain

The problem isn't just about losing good candidates—it's also about the operational inefficiencies caused by manual processing. Recruitment teams spend countless hours on repetitive tasks, such as manually screening resumes and responding to a flood of nonserious applicants.

Sluggish hiring can increase the risk of losing top talent to faster competition. This is particularly damaging in the service industry, where employee availability directly impacts customer satisfaction and business performance. For example, a restaurant with understaffed shifts may experience slower service and lower customer satisfaction, leading to negative reviews and potential revenue loss.

The Domino Effect of Delays

The inefficiencies don't stop at resume review. Once the initial screening drags on, the entire recruitment process becomes a cycle of bottlenecks. Teams face scheduling conflicts for interviews and prolonged decision-making as managers juggle competing priorities. In a busy service industry environment, where peak hours or seasonal demands must be managed, waiting for multiple stakeholders to align can become another obstacle, further extending the timeline.

This results in more than just frustrated candidates, leading to disengagement and drop-offs. According to Half (2016), nearly 60% of candidates drop out of hiring processes that take longer than 4 weeks. For a company dependent on reliable customer service staff, such losses can have a lasting impact on business operations and team morale. Thus, a slow hiring process can quickly become a significant liability in an industry that thrives on speed and efficiency.

Real Hidden Cause: No Skin in the Game

In today's streamlined job market, quick application processes have made it all too easy for unqualified or disinterested candidates to flood the hiring pipeline. This low barrier to entry burdens recruiters, who must sift through countless unsuitable applicants, slowing down the process and undermining hiring quality.

Low Barrier to Application

The click-to-apply trend has significantly impacted service industry hiring, flooding recruiters with applications from candidates who often lack the required experience or genuine interest in the role.

This trend is incredibly challenging for retail, hospitality, or customer service roles. Consider the case of a busy restaurant looking to hire a new server. With online platforms making it easy to apply to multiple positions in minutes, the hiring manager might receive hundreds of applications within a day. Yet, when they dig into the resumes, they find that many of these candidates either need more relevant experience or live too far away to commit to the job reasonably. This sheer volume slows the process, making finding suitable applicants who genuinely want the role harder.

Major retail chains also experience the same strain. One store manager for a national retailer reported receiving over 800 applications for an entry-level sales associate role in a week. After hours of sorting through them, it turned out that nearly 70% of the candidates didn't meet the basic requirements, such as availability to work on weekends. This experience is echoed across the industry, as hiring managers dedicate hours, or even days, to weeding out applicants who never should have applied in the first place.

The issue is that many jobseekers apply to positions indiscriminately, hoping that something will stick.

Quick hiring is crucial in the service industry since it frequently depends on seasonal or part-time employees. Suppose a retail store needs to staff up for the holiday season. In that case, every delay caused by sifting through unqualified candidates means lost sales opportunities. For a hospitality business gearing up for a busy tourist season, extended hiring timelines can lead to a short-staffed team during peak demand. In these scenarios, overwhelmingly unsuitable candidates can paralyze the hiring process, leaving businesses scrambling to fill roles at the last minute.

Minimal Applicant Investment

Another downside to an easy application process is that it often results in minimal investment from candidates. Job seekers have increasingly adopted the "scattergun" approach, applying to as many positions as possible, often without tailoring their applications to the roles they're pursuing.

When you don't have to put in much effort to apply, it's tempting to take this route, but that comes at a cost—both for the applicant and the recruiter. Many candidates aren't researching the companies they're applying to, or worse, they aren't even reading the full job descriptions. As a result, their resumes lack personalization and don't reflect genuine interest in the role. This "spray and pray" method of job hunting might lead to more interview invites for the candidate, but it usually means less commitment.

Skin in the Game

When someone puts in minimal effort to apply, they're more likely to lack enthusiasm or understanding of the role regarding interviews. Imagine you're a recruiter who has finally narrowed down a large applicant pool, only to find that many candidates didn't do their homework before the interview. It often feels like you're wasting time and effort. Hiring managers notice interviewees arriving unprepared, highlighting how this lack of preparation has become a recurring problem.

Consequences for Recruiters

When you're dealing with hundreds of applications for a single role, the task of filtering out nonserious candidates can feel overwhelming. While having more applicants may seem promising initially, it quickly becomes a resource drain, leading to burnout and inefficiencies. This challenge impacts your ability to attract top talent and your organization's finances and team morale. Let's explain how inefficient hiring practices waste valuable resources and why refining your recruitment process is essential for long-term success.

Wasted Resources on Nonserious Candidates

Studies show that recruiting the wrong candidate can cost organizations 30% of the employee's annual salary due to productivity losses, turnover, and rehiring costs (Schooley, 2024). When HR teams receive hundreds of indiscriminate applications, they waste valuable time and money on tasks that don't contribute to an effective hiring process.

Need for Process Optimization

Overall, the negative impacts of a prolonged hiring process can be far-reaching. They affect employee morale, reduce productivity, and damage the company's public image.

Implementing efficient recruitment strategies involves ensuring that the candidates who move through the pipeline are genuinely interested in and suited for the role. Achieving this requires clearly understanding what you're looking for from the outset and using tools and techniques to eliminate wasted time and resources on unqualified or uncommitted applicants.

Companies can significantly reduce wasted effort and costs by refining job descriptions to be highly specific and using technology to prefilter candidates based on genuine interest.

A leaner, more targeted recruitment ensures that the company's recruitment process supports its recruiting volume and speed. Organizations with optimized recruitment processes can make quality hires and experience faster time-to-fill rates than companies without structured systems. Such data-driven methods can help the company grow stronger with the right people in the right roles.

This evidence underscores the importance of reevaluating and refining recruitment strategies to prevent valuable resources from being squandered on nonserious candidates. Recruiters should only invest time in candidates with skin in the game. You'll learn more about skin in the game in Chapter 10.

Key Takeaways

- High application volumes create bottlenecks that extend hiring timelines, frustrating both candidates and HR teams.

- Slow hiring processes result in losing top candidates, who often pursue other opportunities when there are delays.

- Manual resume screening in the service industry drains resources. It can lead to inefficiencies that affect team morale and customer satisfaction.

- Easy-to-apply systems attract unqualified applicants, overwhelm recruiters, and slow hiring genuinely interested candidates.

- Streamlining recruitment with precise job descriptions and technology helps focus on committed candidates, improving hiring speed and quality.

The cost of a chaotic hiring process goes beyond wasted resources—it can also introduce hidden biases. When recruiters are overwhelmed, great candidates may slip through the cracks simply because they don't fit a predefined mold. Let's uncover how these unseen biases can lead to overlooked potential.

Chapter 7:

The Unseen Bias—When

Promising Applicants Fail

Imagine you're interviewing a candidate who ticks every box: outstanding credentials, solid experience, and a personality that lights up the room. You're confident you've struck gold. Fast-forward three months, and the person's struggling, disengaged, and ready to quit. Hidden biases during the hiring process made you overlook the subtle red flags in their communication style that didn't align with the team dynamics. You thought you hired a star but ended up with a misfit.

This leads us to the problem of high turnover of these seemingly great hires—the classic surface issue recruiters often face.

The Surface Problem: High Turnover of Promising Hires

High turnover of promising hires often stems from a gap between expectations set during hiring and the realities of the role. When prioritizing technical skills and qualifications over cultural fit and adaptability, candidates may underperform or leave prematurely, leading to team frustration and costly business disruptions.

Unexpected Underperformance

Sometimes, a candidate seems perfect during the hiring process, only to struggle and underperform once on the job. For example, you might bring on a promising hire with strong technical skills, only to be surprised that they need more flexibility or problem-solving abilities for real-world challenges. One-dimensional assessments focusing on job-specific skills can miss the softer, nuanced traits determining how well someone adapts to complex environments.

Such scenarios aren't just frustrating; they're also costly. High turnover of underperforming hires can severely impact performance and operational efficiency. For business owners and HR professionals, these unexpected underperformances often signal that traditional hiring methods fail to assess the right mix of skills and cultural alignment.

Early Departures Post-Hiring

Early departures post-hiring can significantly hurt the company and the team's morale.

Misalignment in Job Expectations

When a promising hire leaves prematurely, it impacts the bottom line and morale.

Why does this happen so frequently? A significant cause is that the hiring process did not honestly communicate the role's responsibilities and expectations. When the day-to-day reality of the job doesn't match the new employee's expectations, disengagement is almost inevitable.

The Impact of Poor Cultural Fit

Another culprit is poor cultural fit. Even when candidates meet all technical requirements, if their values or work style clash with the company's culture, they're more likely to feel disconnected and unmotivated.

For instance, a high-energy, competitive sales associate might not thrive in a more collaborative and laid-back environment. Mismatches between role expectations and reality can be a significant driver of turnover.

Surprises of New Hires' Performance: Systemic Issues in Recruitment

Even the most thorough hiring process can reveal surprises in a new hire's performance. These surprises often stem from gaps between what candidates present during the interview process and how they behave on the job. While recruiters aim to identify the right fit, unforeseen challenges in attitude, character, and job expectations can still arise, exposing systemic issues in recruitment practices.

Surprises in Attitude

A candidate who seemed upbeat and motivated in interviews may display a different attitude once hired. They might struggle with workplace stress, show resistance to feedback, or disengage over time. This shift can reflect unmet expectations or discomfort with company culture—factors that may not surface during interviews. It highlights the importance of assessing adaptability and intrinsic motivation beyond first impressions.

Surprises in Character

Character traits such as integrity, teamwork, and resilience can be complex to measure accurately during hiring. A new hire who initially appeared cooperative might face challenges with collaboration or accountability in real work situations.

These character mismatches reveal that interviews alone cannot capture the complexities of day-to-day behavior. Behavioral assessments, reference checks, or scenario-based interviews can help address this blind spot.

Surprises in Job Expectations

New hires sometimes bring unrealistic expectations about their role, leading to early frustrations or misalignment. They may expect rapid career progression, lighter workloads, or more flexibility than the job offers. These mismatches often occur when job descriptions aren't clear or during onboarding when expectations aren't aligned.

It emphasizes transparency during recruitment and thorough communication about roles and responsibilities.

Addressing these surprises requires a shift toward more holistic hiring practices—ones that evaluate candidates not just for skills but also for cultural fit, EQ, and realistic job alignment. Proactive steps like more transparent communication, better assessment tools, and structured onboarding can reduce these challenges and improve long-term outcomes for both new hires and employers.

Why do some promising hires fail so spectacularly? The reasons often lie beneath the surface, revealing how people make decisions. Uncovering these hidden causes is crucial for turning the tide on turnover and ensuring new employees succeed in the long run. Let's dig into these underlying issues next.

Real Hidden Causes

Recruitment decisions often fall prey to biases and misguided confidence, leading to hiring mismatches and high turnover. Hidden challenges in candidate assessments, such as lapses in decision hygiene, bias, and overconfidence, undermine hiring quality and employee retention.

Decision Hygiene Lapses

The biggest issue behind decision hygiene lapses is that surprises in a new hire's attitude, character, skills, or job expectations can derail their success early on. When these hidden challenges surface, they often lead to frustration and a fast breakdown during training. Even with the best intentions, a poor fit in these areas makes it hard for the new hire and the company to thrive.

Decision hygiene is a practice that helps you make better hiring decisions by reducing noise and bias. It's about applying structure and consistency to assessing candidates, ensuring emotions, unconscious preferences, or environmental factors don't cloud your judgment. Good decision hygiene means you actively minimize hiring mistakes by prioritizing precise and objective evaluations instead of relying on hope.

Maintaining high decision hygiene—ensuring structured, unbiased evaluations—is vital in recruitment. Lapses in decision hygiene can stem from rushing through assessments or letting biases cloud judgment, which, unfortunately, impacts hiring quality. One of the common pitfalls occurs when overconfidence in a candidate's qualifications skews the assessment process. For example, hiring managers might focus heavily on academic achievements or prestigious work experiences, assuming they indicate overall competence. However, this approach often neglects critical elements like adaptability or cultural fit. Overemphasizing formal qualifications can blind recruiters to potential misalignment with company values or team dynamics.

Organizations often sacrifice decision hygiene to fill vacancies quickly in high-turnover industries like hospitality or healthcare. When a recruiting process is not airtight in minimizing noise and bias, recruiters often miss important traits, increasing the chances of hiring unsuitable candidates. Recruiting noise and bias create a cycle of hiring issues, resulting in higher rates of turnover and lower employee satisfaction.

You'll learn more about decision hygiene in Chapter 13.

The Paradox of Confidence in Hiring

Overconfidence in perceived qualifications creates a paradox for recruiters.

The halo effect is particularly prominent in recruiting, where initial impressions carry significant weight. A candidate who exudes confidence during the interview might appear highly competent yet lack problem-solving abilities essential for success. This overconfidence results in tunnel vision, causing decision-makers to focus solely on the positive qualities while downplaying potential weaknesses.

Long-term retention shows the ripple effect of overconfidence. When hiring based on skewed criteria, organizations often find that seemingly perfect hires leave sooner than expected. Shifting focus from confidence-based impressions to structured assessments of soft skills could mitigate this issue.

Unconscious Bias in Recruitment

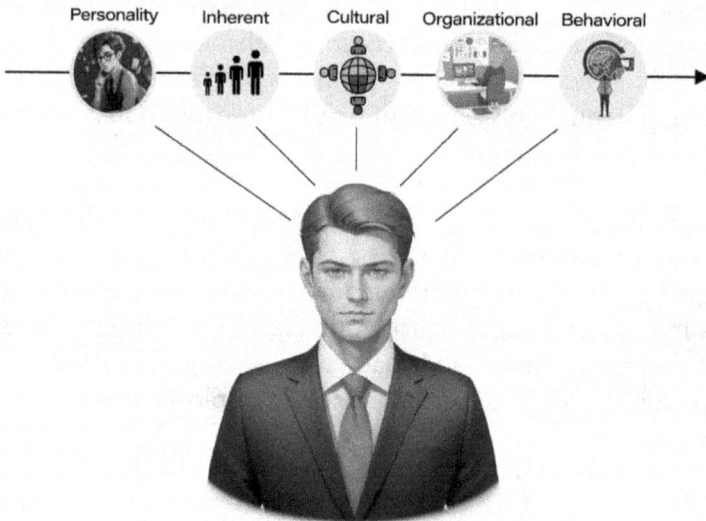

Unconscious biases can make the recruitment process even more complicated. They manifest in subtle ways, affecting how you perceive and evaluate candidates. Unconscious bias may result from personality, inherent, cultural, organizational, and behavioral issues as shown in the figure above.

Besides the halo effect, other common biases include confirmation bias, the primacy effect, the recency effect, and affinity bias. Each distorts judgment differently, often leading to flawed hiring outcomes.

Confirmation Bias

Recruiters demonstrate confirmation bias when they look for details that align with their first impressions of a candidate. If you perceive a candidate as competent from the start, you might subconsciously emphasize their strengths and overlook their weaknesses.

This bias can be particularly harmful when coupled with a high-stakes hiring decision, as it narrows the focus to validating your gut feeling rather than objectively assessing the candidate's complete profile.

Primacy Effect

The primacy effect is another bias where first impressions disproportionately influence your view of the candidate throughout the hiring process. Imagine a candidate who stumbles during the opening of an interview but later showcases solid analytical skills. Because of the initial slip-up, you might unfairly judge them as underqualified. This effect is especially prevalent in interviews, where initial nervousness is mistaken for a lack of competence.

Recency Effect

Similarly, the recency effect emphasizes the most recent interactions, often causing you to overrate or underrate a candidate based on the last few moments of an interview.

If a candidate ends on a solid note, they might leave an impression that overshadows earlier poor performance. This bias can hinder balanced evaluations unless you use a structured review process that assesses performance throughout the interview.

Affinity Bias

Lastly, affinity bias can cause you to favor candidates with similar backgrounds or interests. While this might feel natural, it can inadvertently create a homogeneous team lacking diverse perspectives. This tendency creates significant challenges when building a diverse and inclusive workplace. The presence of affinity bias often leads to a focus on cultural fit, which can undermine efforts to bring in new ideas and varied experiences.

Addressing these biases isn't simple. It requires conscious effort and a systematic approach to candidate evaluation. Combining structured interviews and blind recruitment strategies can significantly reduce bias. In high-turnover industries, especially retail and hospitality, embedding objective assessment tools within the hiring process has improved employee retention by focusing on consistent metrics rather than intuition or surface-level impressions.

Now that you've seen how lapses in decision hygiene and unconscious biases can derail the recruitment process, it's time to look at how you can improve hiring decisions. By refining evaluation methods and implementing fairer assessments, recruiters can reduce turnover, enhance candidate experience, and build stronger teams. Let's delve into these strategies in the next section.

Improving Hiring Decisions

Improving hiring decisions requires a combination of self-awareness and structured processes. Recognizing personal biases and implementing consistent evaluation methods creates a fairer and more transparent recruitment process. Embracing data-driven insights and leveraging AI tools further enhances these efforts, allowing you to make objective, well-informed hiring choices.

Recognizing Personal Biases

Understanding and identifying personal biases is crucial for achieving fairness in candidate evaluation. These biases often influence decisions subtly, shaping outcomes without you even noticing. The tricky part is that these biases operate under the radar, shaping perceptions and judgments. By acknowledging them, recruiters and HR leaders can start counteracting their effects.

You must stay vigilant to prevent bias. It's not always easy, but these steps will help you catch unconscious patterns before they impact your hiring decisions.

Accept That You Have Biases

It's normal to have biases—everyone does. The goal isn't to pretend you're immune to them but to recognize that they exist. By acknowledging this upfront, you're already making progress toward better decision-making. Owning your biases doesn't make you a lousy recruiter; it makes you better because you're willing to grow and improve.

Understand What Triggers Your Biases

Biases don't arise from anywhere—they often respond to particular situations, environments, or moods. Notice when you find yourself unusually attracted to or hesitant about a candidate. Is it their background, education, or how they present themselves? Once you know what triggers your bias, you can disrupt those automatic thoughts and make decisions with more clarity.

These strategies will help you remain grounded and intentional throughout the hiring process. The more you practice self-awareness, the better you'll become at spotting and minimizing bias before it affects your judgment. By staying alert and holding yourself accountable, you'll create a fairer hiring environment—and, ultimately, find the best talent for the job.

Implementing Structured Evaluation

So, how do you keep biases from seeping into your hiring decisions? One powerful way is through structured evaluation frameworks. Structured methods evaluate each candidate using consistent criteria rather than depending on gut instincts or first impressions. This strategy reduces the impact of unconscious biases and creates a fairer process for all applicants.

Using Consistent Assessment Grids

Structured Interviews

Set questions that have been designed in advance

Focus on core competencies of the role

Interviewer knows what to look for from each questions

Questions asked in the same order

Scoring based on consistent criteria

Can go off-script, but will always return

Let's say you're interviewing for a project manager role. Without a structured process, you might emphasize a candidate's confidence and verbal fluency, which cultural background or personal style could influence. However, with a consistent assessment grid, you can objectively compare each candidate on relevant factors like problem-solving ability, leadership experience, and past project outcomes. You're not just relying on what feels impressive now; you have a consistent data set to compare applicants on an apple-to-apple basis.

Leveraging Consistent Scoring Criteria

Imagine having a predefined scoring system for evaluating responses. Instead of scribbling random notes or assigning arbitrary scores, you rate each answer based on specific criteria. This takes subjective judgment out of the equation. Even if a candidate charms you with their personality, their rating will reflect whether they meet the necessary job requirements.

By incorporating these frameworks, you reduce the impact of biases and create a more transparent and fair process. Candidates appreciate clarity and consistency. Knowing what to expect and how others evaluate them lowers anxiety and builds trust. This enhances your employer brand and enables you to attract a diverse talent pool. Most importantly, a consistent and structured process minimizes biases and enhances hiring success.

Using Data Insights and AI

In today's digital age, leveraging data insights and AI tools is essential for minimizing subjectivity in recruitment. AI algorithms objectively analyze large datasets, identifying patterns that human evaluators often overlook. As noted in the Harvard Business Review, tools like AI-driven resume screeners and candidate-matching software outperform humans in applicant screening by at least 25% (Chen, 2023). This advantage stems from AI's ability to consistently apply consistent criteria without being swayed by personal preferences or biases.

Hilton's Success Story: Streamlining Recruitment With AI

Hilton, a well-known leader in the service industry, uses AI to streamline its recruitment process and improve the candidate experience. Hilton developed an AI-powered chatbot to answer candidate queries, provide personalized feedback, and help schedule interviews. This tool improves efficiency and ensures candidates receive timely responses, reducing the typical time-to-hire from 43 days to just 5 days (Thammala, 2023). By handling high-volume recruitment needs in a fraction of the time, Hilton's use of AI has significantly boosted its hiring efficiency and reduced the administrative burden on HR teams.

Implementing these practices requires ongoing education and clear guidelines. For recruiters, workshops on bias awareness and training on AI tools can help them maximize the benefits while minimizing risks. By modernizing your hiring process, you foster fairness and position your organization as a forward-thinking employer that values diversity, objectivity, and efficiency.

Key Takeaways

- High turnover often arises when recruiters prioritize technical skills over cultural fit, leading to early disengagement and costly business disruptions.

- Misalignment between job expectations and reality can result in promising hires underperforming and leaving, impacting team morale and productivity.

- Decision hygiene lapses and biases, such as overconfidence and unconscious bias, can cloud judgment and lead to misaligned hires.

- Structured evaluations and data-driven insights help recruiters assess candidates objectively, reducing the impact of biases in hiring.

- Using AI in recruitment, such as Hilton's AI chatbot, can enhance hiring efficiency and improve the candidate experience by streamlining processes and reducing time-to-hire.

Now that we've explored the hidden pitfalls in hiring and how biases can derail the best intentions, it's time to address the well-meaning but often misguided solutions companies turn to. Sometimes, these quick fixes do more harm than good, creating new problems rather than solving the old ones.

Chapter 8:

Misguided Remedies—Common

Solutions That Worsen the Problem

You know that feeling when your friend tries to fix your computer by randomly clicking things? They swear they're "helping," but before you know it, your screen's upside down, and now your printer's spitting out hieroglyphics. Sometimes, a quick fix turns a tiny glitch into a full-blown catastrophe.

When recruiting for a service company, overloading yourself with more hours and extra effort can feel like the obvious solution. But if you're missing a clear strategy, it's like hitting the gas in the wrong direction—only leading to more burnout. So, how can you work smarter instead of just harder?

Overworking Without Strategic Change

When faced with recruitment challenges, the instinct to "just work harder" might seem like the answer, but it's rarely effective. Without addressing deeper strategic issues, increased effort can quickly lead to burnout, frustration, and the same recurring problems, trapping teams in a cycle of diminishing returns.

The Futility of Simply Working Harder

Instead of taking a step back to analyze the root cause of poor results, many HR professionals throw more hours at the issue, believing that increased effort alone will somehow turn the tide.

Rowing harder doesn't help if the boat is headed in the wrong direction.

- Kenichi Ohmae -

For example, a recruitment team in the service industry might face challenges in finding candidates who are a good fit for open positions. If a recruiter's placements aren't hitting the mark, management might suggest extending work hours or increasing the number of interviews. However, the issue could be an outdated recruiting system that is badly underperforming. The extra hours without addressing that strategic gap leads to burnout, not better results.

Why Overworking Won't Fix Structural Issues

Working harder often means ignoring the bigger picture. When teams operate under intense pressure, they focus on the immediate task rather than the long-term strategy. Recruitment teams caught in this cycle may continue filling positions temporarily without addressing why turnover is so high in the first place. This approach fails to identify the real problem—a dire need for process optimization.

The service industry often experiences this issue during seasonal hiring surges. Companies might push recruiters to work longer hours to handle the influx. Still, the same bottlenecks reappear each year without revisiting the recruitment strategy. Implementing more thoughtful workforce planning or better candidate assessment methods would yield better results, but overwork distracts from such solutions. As a result, recruiters find themselves in the same stressed position year after year.

In his book *The Mythical Man-Month*, Fred Brooks illustrated how adding more hours or workforce doesn't speed up complex projects like software development (Keller, 2022). The recruitment industry sees similar dynamics—more hours without systemic change only complicate the process further. Agile methodologies in tech showed that strategic realignment can often resolve delays and inefficiencies more effectively than throwing more resources at the problem. This lesson applies just as well in recruitment and team management.

Moving Beyond Hard Work

All this evidence underscores that increased effort alone won't solve recruitment challenges in the service industry. Ignoring systemic issues in favor of longer hours is like doubling down on a losing strategy. While effort and dedication are undeniably valuable, they must be aligned with a clear plan and thoughtful planning to make a real impact.

When hard work doesn't cut it, some organizations panic and switch to desperate hiring practices to fill gaps quickly. But this, too, can backfire, leading to long-term damage. Let's examine how these hasty recruitment decisions can create more problems than they solve.

Desperate Hiring Practices

Desperate hiring practices often arise from the pressure to fill vacancies quickly. Still, these short-term fixes can lead to significant long-term problems. Lowering standards, offering temporary incentives, or appearing overly eager to candidates may seem like quick solutions. Still, they can result in poor hires, increased turnover, and a weakened organizational culture.

Lowering Standards to Fill Positions

When companies compromise on candidate qualifications, it often decreases productivity and efficiency. For instance, during recruitment crunches, sectors like healthcare and law enforcement have been known to ease specific hiring requirements to meet immediate staffing needs. This might help in the short run but has a detrimental impact on performance and organizational culture over time. According to a study by the Institute of Labor Economics, companies that opt for faster hiring tend to lower hiring standards and offer more generous wages (Carillo-Tudela et al., 2020). Still, this approach reduces overall efficiency and damages the ability to attract top talent in the long run.

In the service industry, where customer interactions and service delivery are fundamental, lower hiring standards can lead to subpar customer experiences. This not only disrupts daily operations but also damages the company's reputation. An estimated quarter of American employers have adjusted their hiring criteria by skipping standard checks or removing experience requirements, particularly in entry-level positions.

This trend might fill positions faster, but it ultimately introduces a higher likelihood of turnover, costing companies more in rehiring, retraining, and substantial opportunity costs.

Offering Bonuses for Accepting Offers

Some companies turn to short-term incentives like signing bonuses to entice candidates quickly. On the surface, this is a quick way to solve staffing shortages. However, these perks can backfire by attracting candidates more interested in the reward than the role itself.

Some candidates who accepted roles with signing bonuses left their positions after a few months. Why? Because the incentive was the initial attraction, not the job. This scenario is even more common in industries where the work can be demanding, such as retail or hospitality, where a signing bonus might temporarily boost applicant interest but fails to guarantee long-term commitment. These candidates often disengage without a genuine interest in the role, leading to increased turnover rates and decreased morale among long-standing employees.

Furthermore, candidates motivated primarily by monetary rewards may not align with the company's core values, causing team friction and undermining the overall work culture.

Zappos's approach flips the typical bonus strategy by offering new trainees a financial incentive to quit during onboarding. Known as The Offer, Zappos paid $2,000 to those willing to leave (Why Zappos' Training, 2020). This offer is extended after a week or two into its intensive four-week training program, giving new hires time to experience the company's culture and assess whether it's the right fit for them.

This strategy ensures that only those genuinely committed to Zappos's mission and culture stay. Employees who decline the offer demonstrate a higher level of engagement, resulting in a more vital, more motivated workforce. This method minimizes the risk of hiring people not aligned with company values and reduces future turnover costs by identifying potential misfits early on. In essence, Zappos invests in culture alignment rather than using financial perks as bait to attract or retain talent, contrasting sharply with the traditional signing bonus approach many companies take in industries with high turnover, such as retail or hospitality.

Being Too Eager in Front of Job Applicants

In the rush to secure talent, some recruiters go overboard trying to impress candidates. Whether they overpromise benefits, downplay challenges, or neglect thorough screening processes, this eagerness can lead to poor decision-making and mismatches.

For example, to avoid losing candidates to competitors, hiring managers might ignore red flags during interviews or gloss over critical questions. This desperation can lead to hiring individuals who don't fit the role or the company culture, resulting in poor performance and quick turnover. Some companies may bypass traditional screening methods like background checks when desperate to fill roles, a move that often results in higher costs down the line.

This eagerness can also signal instability to candidates, making them wary of joining a company that seems desperate. Being too enthusiastic can draw in candidates who aren't genuinely interested and are just using your eagerness to negotiate better terms. In industries like customer service and hospitality, this can be particularly damaging, as the impact of a poor hire is felt immediately in front-line operations.

So, if settling for less isn't the solution, what about training? Next, let's dive into how poorly allocated training investments can derail the best recruitment intentions.

Misallocated Training Investments

Organizations in the service industry often rely too heavily on training to solve hiring mistakes, hoping it can fill gaps that stem from poor recruitment practices. However, this approach wastes resources and perpetuates a vicious cycle of hiring, turnover, and escalating costs.

Overemphasis on Training Over Recruitment

Relying on training to compensate for hiring mismatches is a costly and ineffective strategy that often misses the mark in developing a capable workforce. In the service industry, aligning recruitment with essential role competencies is key to building a team that can truly excel, without excessive reliance on corrective training.

Why Training Can't Fix Everything

Picture this: a manager hires someone for a customer service role despite clear signs they need interpersonal skills. Instead of reconsidering the decision, the company throws them into intensive training programs, hoping to mold them into a people person. The problem? You're trying to teach a fish to climb a tree. This approach wastes time and resources and ignores the fact that some qualities—like empathy and communication skills—are intrinsic and hard to cultivate later.

This misguided reliance on training as a corrective measure is particularly problematic in the service industry. Recruitment is most effective when it aligns with core competencies and role requirements. However, many agencies still treat training as a fallback rather than a complement to effective hiring practices. This strategy often leads to a workforce that falls short of expectations due to lacking essential qualities needed to excel in their roles.

The Cost of Corrective Training

Using training to fix poor hires affects employee performance and strains company budgets. It simply does not work!

The U.S. Office of Personnel Management found that recruitment and training costs can skyrocket when organizations repeatedly invest in poorly matched employees. Approximately one-third of organizations couldn't estimate how much they spent on remedial efforts (*Recruitment and Retention Strategies*, n.d.).

Imagine this: When you spend money training someone who lacks the skills for the role, that's money taken away from developing employees who are already a great fit and eager to grow. Misallocating training funds disrupts broader strategic initiatives, such as employee engagement and leadership development, limiting their potential impact.

Rethinking the Role of Training

Training should refine existing skills rather than form the entire foundation. It's most effective when it enhances an employee's strengths instead of attempting to fill significant gaps in qualifications. Organizations that rely on training to cover recruitment flaws risk having a workforce that remains underprepared and continually behind.

Organizations can't just rely on training to fix poor hires; they need to get recruitment right from the outset.

Let's explore how overreliance on recruiter judgment can further complicate hiring and lead to even more inefficiencies in building a solid team.

Overreliance on Recruiter's Intuition

Relying solely on intuition in recruitment can feel natural, but it often leads to biased decisions and missed opportunities. Integrating data-driven strategies with instinct allows you to avoid costly hiring mistakes and build a more diverse and innovative team.

Trusting Intuition Over Data in Recruitment

Consider a common scenario: An HR manager might feel a strong instinct about a candidate's potential based on a positive interview. Maybe the candidate was charismatic, seemed to click with the team, or even shared common interests with the hiring manager. Based on this interaction, trusting your gut and pushing forward is tempting. However, this instinct-based decision can overlook critical factors determining long-term success in the role without looking at all the available data, such as previous job performance metrics or project outcomes. And in the recruitment world, those oversights can become expensive mistakes—both financially and in terms of team morale.

The Harvard Business Review found that structured interviews, supported by data, predict future job performance more accurately than unstructured interviews, which tend to be influenced by personal impressions and instincts (Carnahan & Moore, 2023). This insight is especially relevant in the service industry, where success depends on qualities like customer service skills, reliability, and adaptability, which are often hard to identify during a brief interview.

The Hidden Bias in Intuition

Relying on intuition often introduces unconscious bias, which can significantly undermine the quality of new hires.

For example, let's say you're hiring for a service industry role in a customer-facing position. You might instinctively gravitate toward someone who seems personable or reminds you of a previous successful hire. However, this approach could exclude a candidate with a different background or communication style who may be equally, if not more, qualified for the position. The problem with this kind of bias is that it often fails with a quick training failure or a turnover.

You'll get a better understanding of intuition in Chapter 12.

Ignoring Data Leads to Missed Opportunities

If you ignore evidence-based recruitment techniques, you miss valuable insights that could improve your hiring outcomes. Data-driven methods such as analyzing past performance metrics and benchmarking candidate qualifications offer a clearer picture of what works and what doesn't. These methods are instrumental in the service industry, where the stakes are high, and turnover rates are often above average compared to other sectors.

For instance, you might believe that hiring someone with a certain level of experience in customer service guarantees success in the role. However, you might be missing key factors that could predict the candidate's success without looking at data from previous hires, such as how long they stayed in the position or how they performed in customer satisfaction surveys. Using the data at your disposal could significantly reduce turnover and ensure you're hiring employees who are a better fit for your organization.

Imagine you have access to historical data on the characteristics of successful hires for a particular role. Let's say the data reveals that candidates with a score above eight in problem-solving skills, rather than just above seven scores in customer service skills, always thrive in your company. By analyzing this information, you can adjust your hiring criteria to match better the skills that predict long-term success.

In the service industry, where day-to-day tasks often involve interacting with various customers, data-driven recruitment can highlight patterns your intuition might miss. For example, data may reveal that candidates who demonstrate high EQ or adaptability tend to perform better under stress, leading to higher customer satisfaction and retention rates.

Key Takeaways

- Pushing yourself without a clear recruitment strategy often leads to burnout and recurring issues instead of meaningful results. Working harder without direction only perpetuates problems, leaving you with a cycle of short-term fixes rather than sustainable improvements.

- Lowering hiring standards or offering signing bonuses in a rush to fill positions frequently results in poor hires and long-term inefficiencies. These quick fixes often come back to haunt you, as underqualified hires impact team performance and add hidden costs over time.

- When organizations use training funds to correct poor hiring choices, they waste valuable resources that could support broader development initiatives. Investing in candidates who aren't the right fit restricts growth opportunities for other employees. It weakens the overall impact of training programs.

- When recruiters rely too much on intuition, they can introduce bias and overlook critical data, resulting in costly hiring errors. Making decisions without data increases the risk of choosing candidates based on assumptions rather than solid evidence, which can weaken team performance.

- Data-driven recruitment strategies help pinpoint indicators of long-term success, reduce turnover, and build a stronger team in the service industry. Using data, you can align hires closely with company goals and create a more stable, productive workforce.

When overworking and gut instincts only lead to burnout and poor hires, it's time to rethink your approach. Instead of exhausting your team and relying on chance, there's a more thoughtful way to get better results. Next, let's explore a breakthrough strategy for improving recruitment.

Chapter 9:

The Breakthrough Strategy—A

Revolutionary Recruitment

Solution

If you're a recruiter, you've likely faced several issues that make hiring a steep uphill battle. Some seemingly "great solutions" to recruitment challenges—like working harder, lowering hiring standards, increasing training time, or putting more confidence in a recruiter's instinct—often backfire. These approaches frequently worsen the situation, ultimately aggravating the issue rather than addressing it. Working harder without a clear strategy can lead to burnout, and lowering standards risks bringing in candidates who aren't fully qualified, increasing turnover and training demands. Overrelying on intuition can also introduce bias and noise, derailing efforts to find the best fit.

These "fixes" compound the problem instead of providing meaningful improvement.

Here's where the breakthrough strategy comes in—a solution that targets these pains directly and smartly. Instead of putting all the pressure on recruiters and relying on outdated tactics, it's about rethinking the process from the ground up. It is about a revolution. This strategy focuses on efficiency, clarity, and effectiveness, transforming recruitment into a well-oiled machine that delivers results. Let's break free from the chaos and explore a revolutionary approach that tackles these pain points head-on.

With that in mind, let's examine the overview of the comprehensive solution that transforms this chaos into a high-performing recruiting system.

Overview of the Comprehensive Solution

To ensure a recruitment process that's both efficient and effective, you need a revolutionary strategy. Let's break down the key components:

- A skin-in-the-game recruitment process helps filter out unqualified candidates by giving them fundamental tasks, ensuring only motivated applicants advance.

- Striking a balance between candidate screening and advocacy allows recruiters to evaluate qualifications while rigorously promoting the role to promising candidates.

- Leveraging data insights aids recruitment by identifying effective platforms, tracking candidate success, and predicting which applicants may thrive.

- Maintaining decision hygiene with structured templates and objective scoring prevents bias and supports fair and effective hiring aligned with long-term goals.

- AI technology enhances recruitment by accelerating resume screening, reducing bias, and improving hiring consistency without replacing human judgment.

With these strategies in place, your recruitment process becomes more efficient and effective at bringing in the right talent. You optimize the process while keeping quality at the forefront, positioning your business for lasting success.

Now, let's shift gears to the skin-in-the-game recruiting process. You'll learn how to implement a skin-in-the-game process to root out unqualified and unfit job candidates with almost no extra work, saving time, money, and stress!

Skin-In-The-Game Recruiting Process

Skin-in-the-game recruiting is about rooting out unqualified candidates quickly, without extra work! By integrating tailored assessments and realistic job previews, you can screen out unqualified applicants rapidly, ensuring that only serious and invested candidates move forward—saving time, money, and resources in high-turnover industries.

Job Design: Creating Attractive Opportunities

A well-thought-out job design shapes how appealing your opportunity will be. By clearly defining job expectations and responsibilities, you attract candidates who fit the role well. This clarity is crucial in the service industry, with high turnover and specific demands. It helps filter out applicants not aligned with your goals, leaving you with genuinely interested candidates.

Making the Job More Appealing

In a competitive market, making your job stand out often involves flexible offerings. While some job requirements are nonnegotiable (like shift timings), there are aspects you can adapt to boost appeal, like remote work options or flexible start times. This flexibility can make all the difference.

Understanding Applicant Segments

Recognizing what different applicants value allows you to design a job that speaks to them. Millennials may prefer career progression, while Gen Z prioritizes work–life balance. Customizing your outreach for each group boosts engagement, making candidates feel seen and valued.

Meeting Candidate Expectations Through Customization

Offering competitive pay, flexible schedules, personalized benefits, and growth opportunities goes a long way. Employees want more than just a paycheck—they want a future. Customizing your offer shows your company is ready to invest in its growth and well-being.

Does this cost too much?

No, these changes don't cost too much. The price of not making your job attractive compared to competitors is far higher.

Use Applicant Commitment and Professionalism to Screen Out Unqualified Applicants, Fast!

Screening or commitment and professionalism allows you to identify candidates who may need to be more serious, have enough interests, or are emotionally fit for the job. For instance, asking an applicant a simple question via SMS about the last job's travel time and testing how fast the response is or if the applicant responds can detect if the interest in the job is genuine. Implementing a "skin-in-the-game" recruiting approach with a self-veto option allows candidates to reveal their genuine interest in the position naturally and efficiently.

You can create a system that allows candidates to self-veto if they aren't genuinely committed, relieving recruiters from manually evaluating every applicant. You accomplish this by establishing small, reasonable tasks that gradually filter out those who lack interest or qualifications. Here's how you can structure these checkpoints:

Establish Simple but Telling Tasks

Introduce small but purposeful tasks to gauge candidate commitment at each stage of the application pipeline. These could include

- **Completing a two-minute survey:** This brief survey could ask about availability, interest level, or work-related scenarios.

- **Answering two questions via SMS:** You can automate this step to check responsiveness. Serious applicants will take a minute to reply, showing they're paying attention.

- **Self-evaluating their job fit:** Ask them to rate their fit for the role on a scale from 1 to 7. It's a simple task, but it offers insight into their understanding of the position's demands.

- **Asking a direct question:** Pose an open-ended question relevant to the job. Monitor how promptly and thoughtfully the applicants respond.

Create Self-Veto Opportunity at Every Stage of the Recruiting Pipeline

By including these checkpoints at every step of the hiring process, you give applicants a chance to screen themselves out if they're not entirely on board. For instance, if someone can't handle a simple request like a survey or fails to reply to an SMS message, they've essentially opted out.

This approach quickly eliminates random, unserious, and no-longer-interested applicants. It minimizes the time spent on candidates who lack genuine interest in the role.

Focus Efforts on Committed Candidates

In high-volume recruitment, sifting through hundreds of applications can be overwhelming. Instead of spending hours reviewing resumes, automate a simple question for all candidates. Only the committed ones will respond. After a few rounds of these checkpoints, candidates willing to put in the effort will remain.

At this point, it's time well spent reviewing their qualifications more thoroughly.

Work smarter, not just harder!

Install Checkpoints at Every Stage

Set up these self-veto opportunities at each process stage to maintain this efficiency. Whether during the initial application, interview scheduling, or post-interview tasks, consistent checkpoints will identify those who lack total commitment. This way, your time and energy go toward candidates who are serious about the role and more likely to be a good fit.

With this groundwork set, let's turn to the careful balance between screening candidates and advocating for the role. This topic delves into assessing candidates objectively while firmly and subtly advocating your job's strengths and benefits to qualified job applicants.

The Fine Balance of Screening and Advocating

Finding the right candidate fit for service roles isn't just about evaluating and screening; it's about understanding the wins for applicants from this job based on their needs and desires. This process requires a careful balance of objective assessment and advocacy to ensure you're hiring for technical and interpersonal strengths while promoting the job's strengths and benefits to applicants' needs and desires.

Job Design: Being the Best Option for Your Applicant Segments

Going beyond standard job postings is vital in attracting top talent. Craft roles that appeal directly to different applicant groups' preferences, creating personalized job offerings. Recognizing the unique needs of each segment lets you stand out in a competitive job market.

Defining Applicant Segments

Effective job design starts by categorizing applicants based on demographics, psychographics, and behaviors. Demographic segmentation considers attributes like experience level and location, while psychographics dive deeper, focusing on values and motivations. This lets you design roles that appeal to candidates' priorities, like promoting growth opportunities for career-driven applicants or flexible hours for those seeking balance. Behavioral insights add another layer by tracking habits, such as how some applicants actively engage with social media job ads.

Adapting your strategy around these insights increases engagement and makes your outreach feel more relevant.

Recognizing and Addressing Each Segment's Needs and Desires

Once you've defined segments, align roles to match each group's needs. For example, many applicants in the house cleaning industry prefer weekday hours. Making weekend shifts optional can attract top talent who value work–life balance. Similarly, candidates focused on growth respond well to opportunities for advancement, like structured training programs. By offering these, you will likely see longer employee tenure and higher job satisfaction.

Keeping up with trends helps refine this approach. Gathering feedback from candidates, both successful and unsuccessful, reveals changing expectations. Tools like AI-driven analytics can help identify which roles resonate with specific applicant groups, making it easier to target job ads effectively.

Mapping Out Job Strengths and Challenges by Segment

Recruiting for service roles means understanding each segment's strengths and expectations. Client-facing jobs, for example, can be marketed by highlighting the role's impact on customer experience. In contrast, behind-the-scenes roles may appeal to candidates who value mission-driven work. Transparency around pay is crucial, as competitive salaries attract talent, while flexible shifts appeal to those managing other commitments. Highlighting benefits like health insurance or wellness programs further strengthens your appeal.

Advocating With Emotion First, Then Logic

Connecting with candidates emotionally before using logic can enhance your recruitment messaging. Compelling job descriptions inspire by touching on emotional triggers, such as a sense of purpose or accomplishment. Describe benefits, routine, and how the role fits into candidates' lives. Framing job details to highlight fulfillment helps build a lasting connection, making candidates feel understood and valued.

Advocating for the Job's Strengths and Potential

When advocating for a position, your goal isn't just to fill a vacancy; it's to match the right candidate with the right opportunity. You highlight what makes the job appealing and an excellent fit for an applicant's unique situation. This approach helps attract candidates who genuinely thrive in the role, leading to higher retention and job satisfaction.

Tailoring the Job's Strengths to Candidate Needs

For example, let's say you're hiring for a cleaning technician role. This position offers daytime hours with no night shifts or weekend work. This schedule might seem essential to some, but to a working parent, it could be a game-changer. Many moms are looking for stable jobs that allow them to be at home with their children in the evenings and on weekends.

Advocate for it instead of just listing the hours in the job description! Frame the job as an excellent opportunity for candidates who want a steady routine and more time for their family. You could say, "We understand how important it is to have a schedule that allows you to be there for your family. This position offers flexible daytime hours with no weekends or nights, making it a perfect fit for parents who want a steady job while still having evenings and weekends at home."

Consider Sarah, a single mom looking for work. She had been struggling with a job that demanded inconsistent evening shifts, making it challenging to be present for her kids' homework, dinners, and bedtime routines. During her interview, you highlighted that the cleaning technician role offers predictable daytime hours. Immediately, Sarah sees the benefit—not only does this job give her financial stability, but it also aligns perfectly with her personal life. By advocating the job's strengths, you position it as a win-win situation for Sarah.

Why Advocating Matters

When you advocate for the role's strengths, you help candidates see how the job fits into their lives and solves potential pain points. This attracts quality applicants and shows them you understand their needs and value their well-being. This compassionate approach builds trust and helps candidates envision themselves succeeding in the role.

Remember, advocacy isn't about overselling or exaggerating—it's about aligning the job's strengths with the candidate's values. It's a two-way street that prioritizes the well-being of the company and the employee, leading to more substantial long-term results.

By advocating for the job's strengths and potential, you create an environment where both the role and the candidate succeed.

Balancing Objectivity With Advocacy

When recruiting, you want to showcase your organization's strengths to attract the best candidates. However, leaning too heavily into advocacy—promoting the role or the company too enthusiastically—can backfire. Finding the right balance of objectivity and advocacy is essential for establishing trust and engaging candidates effectively throughout the recruiting pipeline. It's like dating: If you come on too strong, you might end up pushing people away without meaning to.

By being intentional and subtle in your approach, you'll create a more inviting experience for applicants while also making a compelling case for your company.

Too Much Advocacy: The Pitfalls of Overeagerness

Advocacy can easily overwhelm candidates if advocates go overboard, making candidates feel like someone is selling to them rather than inviting them into a potential partnership. This effect, known as the "reactance" response in psychology, occurs when people feel that someone is trying too hard to influence their choices; they may respond by resisting or disengaging.

Think of it this way: If you were on a first date and your companion insisted on talking about their best qualities nonstop, you'd probably lose interest or feel uncomfortable. The same principle applies in recruiting—too much advocacy can seem pushy and off-putting.

Instead, consider a more measured approach. Showcasing your organization's strengths is vital, but do so with balance. Adopting a "firm but subtle" advocacy strategy invites candidates to explore the opportunity without feeling pressured.

For example, rather than overemphasizing perks and benefits upfront, weave these into conversations naturally, aligning them with the candidate's interests or needs as you get to know them better. This way, you present the role and company benefits as part of a broader, two-way conversation rather than a hard sell.

Systematic and Subtle Advocacy at Every Stage

A well-rounded advocacy strategy involves being consistent and nuanced at every step of the recruiting process. This means that rather than reserving advocacy only for the initial stages of recruitment, you integrate it thoughtfully throughout each stage, from the first interaction to the final offer. Whether in screening, interviews, or follow-up discussions, keep your messaging aligned with the candidate's journey through the pipeline.

For example, you might highlight the company's mission and core values in initial calls. As candidates progress, gradually introduce career growth potential, team dynamics, and specific benefits. This approach ensures that advocacy doesn't feel heavy-handed but instead gives candidates a fuller view of what the role and organization offer.

Systematically applying subtle advocacy also creates a cohesive experience across all candidate interactions, reinforcing a positive image of the company without overwhelming them.

With a balanced advocacy strategy in place, the next step involves using data to make even smarter recruiting decisions. By collecting and analyzing insights at each stage of the pipeline, you can identify where candidates engage best and where adjustments improve the recruiting experience further. Let's look at how leveraging data insights can enhance your recruitment process.

Leveraging Data Insights

Data insights have revolutionized recruitment by enabling faster, more objective decision-making. From identifying top talent through AI-driven tools to leveraging predictive analytics for better job–candidate matching, these strategies ensure that recruiters make better, more efficient hiring decisions while promoting diversity and reducing bias.

The Limitations of Intuition in Recruitment

While intuition plays a role in hiring, relying solely on it often invites bias and inconsistency. Research by Dr. Daniel Kahneman shows that structured, data-backed methods offer a more reliable recruitment approach, blending informed intuition with objective insights for better long-term hiring outcomes (Batista, 2021).

Daniel Kahneman's Insights

Nobel laureate Kahneman distinguishes between intuitive, fast judgments and analytical, slow thinking. His findings reveal that while intuition feels right in the moment, it often lacks accuracy. Using structured interviews, Kahneman demonstrated that the Israeli military improved hiring consistency and accuracy, a practice still relevant today.

Understanding Cognitive Biases

Biases like overconfidence and the halo effect can skew judgment. Service industry recruiters often value personality but risk high turnover by favoring "gut feelings" over data. For instance, hiring a candidate based on charm alone might overlook their skill gaps.

Building a Data-Driven Recruitment Pipeline

Creating a data-driven recruitment pipeline combines clearly defined qualifications, thoughtful assessments, and streamlined processes. Data insights can pinpoint top talent and support retention, which is crucial in high-turnover service industries.

Defining Critical Qualification Attributes

In service-focused industries, knowing what attributes matter for each role is essential. For example, effective communication and handling challenging situations are key for retail. At the same time, empathy and precision might be priorities in healthcare. By defining these core attributes, you're laying the groundwork for a recruitment process that finds candidates who truly fit your team.

Developing Assessment Tools

Once you've set qualifications, develop assessments that reflect the job's demands. For instance, a scenario-based test in hospitality can reveal how a candidate would handle a challenging guest. Interviews should dig into past experiences to predict future performance, offering valuable insights into their skills and cultural fit.

Establish Quantified Data Measurements for All Evaluations

Quantify interview responses, application answers, and survey results. Build a recruiting data system to collect and evaluate applicant data consistently.

We show through our experience that we can quantify all recruiting data. Yes. 100% of recruiting data can be quantified. Consistently collected qualitative data is the foundation for obtaining valuable insights.

Data-Driven Decision-Making: Getting Comparable Facts and Optimizing Evaluations Quickly and Accurately

In the fast-paced recruitment world, especially in the service industry, data-driven decision-making is becoming a vital tool for HR professionals. With these strategies, recruiters can streamline evaluations, make objective decisions faster, prevent bias and noise from impacting objectivity, and optimize the hiring process, leading to better candidate matching and overall efficiency.

Using Data for Objective and Fast Decision-Making

Leveraging data analytics allows you to transform candidate data into valuable insights quickly. Tools like ATSs combined with AI-based platforms help you analyze candidate qualifications and work experiences, making comparisons straightforward and accurate.

For example, companies using predictive analytics models can improve hiring efficiency by reducing the time-to-hire and ensuring better candidate matches. Platforms that establish a consistent recruiting pipeline with proven practical interview questions, clear scoring criteria, and self-veto mechanisms can dramatically reduce the time-to-hire and maximize hiring decision quality.

Predictive Analytics: Foreseeing Candidate Success

Predictive analytics relies on historical data to evaluate a candidate's likelihood of succeeding in a particular position. Reviewing previous hiring patterns allows you to identify whether a candidate is a strong match, ultimately enhancing the quality of your hiring choices. Regression analysis, machine learning, and AI prediction models are powerful tools for predictive analytics.

Identifying Recruitment Patterns to Improve Strategies

Analyzing recruitment data helps you identify trends in successful hires and pinpoint areas that need improvement. Starbucks, for example, used data analytics to uncover factors causing high turnover. Based on these insights, they adjusted their recruitment messaging, which improved retention rates and increased employee satisfaction. This method is vital to refining hiring strategies and keeping top talent long-term in high-turnover industries like hospitality.

Enhancing Accuracy and Speed in Assessments

Data-driven assessment tools allow you to evaluate a candidate's skills, behaviors, and cultural fit faster. Companies like Unilever have shifted their focus from traditional resume reviews to analyzing behavioral traits using AI, resulting in a 16% increase in diversity among new hires (*Unleashing AI in Unilever*, 2024). This shift speeds up the process and enhances the precision of candidate evaluations.

Implementing Key Metrics for Success

Tracking critical metrics like time-to-hire, quality of hire, training success rate, and first-year retention rates can provide a clear view of your recruitment process's effectiveness. These insights allow you to sharpen your strategies and improve the hiring process.

Now that you understand the power of data in streamlining recruitment, the next step is ensuring these insights are applied systematically. Implementing decision hygiene—creating a structured and unbiased decision-making process—ensures that data-driven strategies lead to consistent and effective outcomes. Let's explore how to implement decision hygiene in your recruitment practices.

Implementing Decision Hygiene

Reducing bias and noise in hiring is essential for building a diverse and dynamic workforce, especially in the service industry. Implementing strategies like standardized screening, blind hiring, and role-specific criteria can create a fairer evaluation process, leading to more objective hiring decisions and more robust team performance.

Reducing Bias and Noise in Hiring

When you think about reducing bias and noise in hiring, it's not just about fairness—it's also about making more intelligent decisions. Limiting bias helps you avoid hiring the wrong person, leading to better hires, lower turnover, and a stronger team. Let's discuss how reducing bias and noise in the hiring process can lead to long-term success.

Understanding the Impact of Bias and Noise

Bias can take many forms in hiring, from unconscious preferences for candidates who "seem like us" to overvaluing certain traits that don't predict job performance. For example, hiring managers might lean toward candidates with similar backgrounds or interests, even if those qualities don't directly relate to job performance. This can lead to a mismatch, where the person hired isn't the best fit for the role or the company culture, ultimately increasing turnover rates. Reducing bias leads to a fairer hiring process and supports more decisive hiring decisions, positively influencing your team's overall success.

Noise is also a type of error, but unlike bias, it occurs randomly. Bias leads to consistent mistakes in a specific direction. At the same time, noise results in poor hiring outcomes through a different mechanism, requiring alternative solutions.

Better Hires, Lower Turnover

Directly reducing bias improves the quality of your hires. Eliminate distractions like irrelevant preferences and overvalued traits. This approach will yield candidates who fulfill the job's qualifications. It leads to lower turnover, as employees who are well-suited for their roles are more likely to stay and thrive. For instance, a company focusing too much on hiring outgoing personalities might need to pay more attention to introverted candidates who excel in more analytical or detail-oriented roles. Concentrating on essential skills and qualifications helps you build a diverse and impactful team.

Acknowledge Unconscious Bias Exists—And Address It

First, you need to recognize that bias is part of human decision-making. This isn't about placing blame but recognizing how deeply held perceptions can influence decisions. For example, unconscious biases, like favoring candidates with similar backgrounds or relying on "gut feelings," can lead to hiring decisions based more on comfort than actual competence. A Harvard Business School study revealed that unconscious bias often manifests in selecting candidates with shared experiences, such as attending the same school or simply having a similar name (Carnahan & Moore, 2023).

To reduce this, you can be very aware of the triggers of the common biases in recruiting. The halo effect often arises because human perception is not purely objective. Instead of relying solely on factual information, we actively build an impression of others based on previous knowledge, constructing an image that aligns with our beliefs. Knowing these, a recruiter must delay judgment until the end and focus on data collection.

Implementing Structured Interviews

One of the best ways to reduce noise and bias is by standardizing the screening process and asking every candidate the same structured interview questions, which levels the playing field. Structured interviews, where all candidates answer the same questions in the same sequence, lead to fairer evaluations and help reduce the impact of factors like race or gender.

Evaluating interviews using a scoring rubric ensures objectivity and consistency. You can focus on merit instead of personal biases by rating responses based on quantifiable and consistent criteria, such as communication clarity or problem-solving ability.

Collaborative Decision-Making

Blind hiring techniques, such as anonymous voting by a committee, can significantly reduce bias in the hiring process and create a fairer, more inclusive workplace. In blind hiring, recruiters and hiring committees evaluate candidates without personal identifiers—such as name, age, gender, or background—that might trigger unconscious bias. This approach gives each candidate an equal chance, focusing exclusively on their skills and credentials instead of their traits. Google, known for its data-driven recruitment strategies, has explored methods like these to help build diverse teams focused solely on a candidate's qualifications and skills.

Deploying AI Technology

Integrating AI technology into your recruitment process isn't just a trend—it's a game-changer. By leveraging AI, you can streamline hiring, reduce bias, and make better decisions based on data rather than guesswork.

Enhancing Objectivity and Reducing Bias and Noise

AI technology enhances objectivity in hiring by reducing bias and noise. Even with the best intentions, human recruiters can unintentionally let personal biases affect their decisions. Factors like a candidate's name, gender, or age can sometimes shape these biases, impacting the fairness of the hiring process and resulting in missed opportunities for well-qualified individuals.

Enhancing Efficiency and Accuracy

AI significantly enhances efficiency and accuracy, making it ideal for high-turnover industries like retail and hospitality. These tools can quickly sort through hundreds or even thousands of applications in far less time than it would take a human recruiter, allowing you to concentrate on the strategic aspects of hiring. Automating repetitive tasks like resume screening saves time and boosts overall productivity.

Make Much Better Hiring Decisions Based on Facts

Traditional recruitment methods rely on subjective factors like gut instinct or unconscious biases. In contrast, AI helps you make data-backed hiring decisions. With AI systems, you can objectively evaluate resumes based on relevant skills and experiences rather than superficial attributes like educational background or gender. Recruiters believe AI can help eliminate unintentional human biases from hiring, promoting a fairer and more inclusive candidate evaluation.

AI-driven tools identify patterns in successful hires and adjust their criteria with each hiring cycle. The system continuously improves, aligning more closely with your company's unique requirements. As a result, candidates chosen through AI have a higher success rate in passing interviews and receiving job offers than those picked by human recruiters. This process strengthens hiring consistency by ensuring all teams evaluate applicants using the same standards.

Enhance Objectivity and Consistency in Hiring

One of AI's critical strengths in recruitment is its ability to maintain consistency across candidate evaluations. Traditional hiring methods can vary widely depending on who conducts the interview, leading to potential assessment discrepancies. AI offers standardized assessments through tools like natural language processing, which can evaluate interview responses for crucial competencies and traits without letting personal biases creep in. This approach ensures that every candidate is measured against the same benchmarks, leading to more equitable and reliable outcomes.

Regarding diversity, AI tools can help eliminate exclusionary language in job postings. For example, "ninja" or "rock star" may unintentionally deter female candidates. At the same time, more neutral terms like "confident" can appeal to a broader audience. When companies have implemented AI to screen and refine job postings, they've seen increases in diverse hires. This means AI enhances the fairness of your evaluation process and helps attract a wider talent pool.

Cost-Effectiveness

AI doesn't just improve efficiency and accuracy; it's also a smart financial move for your recruitment strategy. By automating repetitive tasks, like initial resume screenings or even scheduling interviews, AI saves you valuable time and labor costs, freeing your team to focus on high-impact tasks that add value. These savings grow over time as the AI system continues refining its processes, reducing the need for extensive human intervention.

Beyond day-to-day savings, AI can offer deeper insights into a candidate's potential for long-term success with your company. With data analysis, AI can predict which candidates will likely stay longer and thrive within your culture, saving you the high cost of turnover and rehiring. Instead of continually recruiting to fill the same positions, you're building a stable, committed team, benefiting your bottom line and organizational culture. By investing in AI, you're investing in a sustainable, cost-effective recruitment strategy that brings lasting value to your business.

Key Takeaways

- A multifaceted and revolutionary approach addresses the service industry recruiters' challenges more effectively.

- Combining commitment strategies with a skin-in-the-game recruiting process, balancing screening and advocating, leveraging data insights, implementing decision hygiene, and deploying AI technology leads to exceptional hiring success.

- Adopting innovation is vital for remaining competitive in talent acquisition.

Now that we've explored how AI enhances efficiency and accuracy in hiring, let's turn our focus to skin-in-the-game recruiting. This strategy isn't just about filling positions—it's about building genuine commitment and ensuring top-quality hires by aligning recruiter and company goals more closely.

Chapter 10:

Skin-In-The-Game Recruiting—

Rooting Out Low Quality, Low

Interest, and Unqualified

Applicants

You post an open position and boom—applications flood in. You feel optimistic until you notice candidates who ignore the job description. One attached a blank cover letter; another failed to attach a resume, clearly stated as a mandatory requirement in the job application form. It's like giving everyone a ticket to the job fair without checking if they care enough to show up in proper shoes. You tighten your screening—by installing an application form with 20 assessment questions. Now, only the serious players get through. Suddenly, it's not just more manageable—it's better. Quality rises when you raise the stakes.

People naturally won't want to enter if what's beyond the gate isn't appealing. We need to ensure what's inside offers good pay, reasonable hours, and benefits, so when a candidate fails to pass through our "gate of professionalism and commitment," we can be confident it's a genuine decision. Rooting out unsuitable candidates becomes a natural part of this process.

This chapter focuses on skin-in-the-game recruiting. This method quickly identifies serious candidates while letting unqualified or uncommitted applicants naturally filter themselves out. You'll discover how small, purposeful tasks, such as quick surveys or response-time checks via SMS, help screen out applicants who aren't wholly interested or prepared for the role. By setting up checkpoints at each stage of the recruitment pipeline, you can save time, energy, and resources by focusing on candidates who demonstrate genuine commitment and professionalism.

This system makes recruitment efficient and ensures you only invest in applicants with "skin in the game."

Job Design: Creating Attractive Opportunities

Job design plays a crucial role in skin-in-the-game recruiting because it ensures that candidates clearly understand the expectations and demands of the role upfront. A well-structured job allows recruiters to identify qualified and committed candidates confidently. When job requirements are precise, particularly in areas such as professionalism and commitment, candidates who self-select out of the process are likely not a good fit for the role.

This approach streamlines recruitment by removing individuals who may not be aligned with the company's goals or values while giving recruiters confidence that those who remain are well-suited to succeed. In essence, a strong job design supports the integrity of the skin-in-the-game method by aligning candidate interests with business needs, ensuring only the best-suited candidates move forward.

To attract top talent, especially in the service industry, you need to cater to the evolving needs of today's workforce. Offering a steady paycheck is no longer enough; employees want meaningful work, growth opportunities, flexibility, and a company culture that aligns with their needs, desires, and values.

Making the Job More Appealing Than Alternatives

Some job requirements are essential and nonnegotiable, such as retail associates needing to work evening and weekend shifts. However, other aspects of a job can be adjusted without affecting core responsibilities, allowing employers to be flexible based on candidates' preferences. For example, offering remote work options or flexible start times can appeal to top talent without compromising essential tasks. By staying open to modifying nonessential features, businesses can create more appealing roles while maintaining productivity.

Creating a job that stands out starts with ensuring it's more appealing than what competitors offer. With the service industry employing about 50% of the global workforce, staying competitive requires employers to provide a work experience that resonates (Mathieu, 2024).

For instance, flexibility has become a significant selling point, with research showing that 54% of workers would leave their current jobs if remote or hybrid work options disappeared (More Than Half, 2021). Offering flexibility, especially in a high-turnover industry like service, can be a game-changer. Employees in these roles often juggle multiple responsibilities, and the ability to control their schedule can make your job offering more attractive.

To further differentiate your role, highlight what sets your company apart. Career development programs, upskilling opportunities, and promoting work–life balance are all strong selling points.

By 2025, employers must align their recruitment strategies with the values and expectations of Millennials and Gen Z, who will likely comprise 75% of the workforce (Timmes, 2022). These generations seek more than a paycheck; they want growth, flexibility, community and environmental impact, and meaningful work. By emphasizing these aspects, you make your job more enticing than alternatives.

Understanding Applicant Segments

Tailoring your job design to attract top talent starts with understanding who your applicants are and what they value. Candidates from different generations and backgrounds bring diverse expectations to the table. Millennials prefer jobs that offer collaboration and career progression. At the same time, Gen Z prioritizes work–life balance and roles with a social impact.

The table below outlines the different applicant segments and their specific needs for the home cleaning technician role.

Advocacy based on Segments

Advocacy Angles	Applicant Segments					
	No Strong Support	With Direct & Strong Support	Student	Inexperienced and Searching	Professional	Experienced
Have	A steady schedule, reliable income. Take good care of family all evenings and weekends. Growth!	Contribute to family finance substantially, while still, have time to spend with family in evening and weekends.	Great income to pay for school. Flexible schedule, a company that supports your school plans. Have weekends off either to take a class or to do homework.	More and steady income and schedule. The opportunity to grow with the company. Have time for self and family. Have a job that can become a career.	Company with integrity, proud, and support. Have steady schedule and no night. Opportunity to grow within the company.	Flexible schedule, secure job, great working environment, great team members, growth opportunity, and good pay.
Feel	Relieve, in control, happy, fulfil	Happy, pride, accomplished	Happy, relief, focused	Earn more, happier, healthier	Secure, kind, valued	Happy, accomplished, healthier
Average day	Work during the day only. In the evenings and weekends, spend time with family.	Secure income, while get home early and still be able to take care of family in the evening and weekends.	Work in the mornings, go to school in the evenings and weekends. Have plenty of time to do homework in the night or weekends.	Earn more. Work during the day time. Flexibility in the evenings and weekends to focus on personal goals!	Only work during the day. Have a schedule every day. Don't have to drive to the office daily.	Work during the day, have the evenings and nights for the family. Not feeling tired. Can grow to higher level.
Status	Successful, super parent	Provider, equality, and independence	Put together, well on the way to complete school successfully	Successful, accomplish	Professional, valued independent, successful	Healthy, strong, in control, and growth
Good Vs. Evil	Don't have to choose between a good income and take care of family. Who said you can't have both?	Both a key income provider to family and GREAT parent! Who said you can't do both?	Don't have to be broke to finish school. Not having to pick between an education and being able to support for self (independence)	Be Successful with an enjoyable job that you can earn more, grow and become happier. Who said you can not have a enjoyable physical job, earn great money, grow professionally, and a career? You can have all three!	You are good at cleaning and you love it. Who said cleaning can not be a respected career? Cleaning is not just a job but could be an amazing career.	Achieve an healthy job and a well paid career. Have both!

Segmenting your applicants based on these values allows you to craft recruitment strategies that speak directly to their motivations. This strategy becomes even more essential for managing the high turnover rates in the service industry. For example, baby boomers might prefer traditional outreach methods like LinkedIn or email. At the same time, marketers can reach Gen Z through platforms like SMS messaging, Instagram, or TikTok. Adjusting your messaging and outreach based on these preferences ensures you connect with potential hires where they are most engaged.

Aligning With Applicant Needs and Desires

Once you understand your candidates' needs and wants, it's time to align your job offerings with their desires. Research shows that nearly half of employees quit their jobs because they do not see enough opportunities for career advancement. In comparison, 44% cite low pay and benefits as primary reasons for departure (Caucci, 2021). In the service industry, where many roles are seen as temporary or transitional, emphasizing growth opportunities can significantly attract and retain talent.

The table below highlights growth opportunities within the home cleaning technician role, showing that even a "cleaning job" can be structured to support employees' growth aspirations and development goals.

Growth Opportunities via 7 Levels of Home Cleaning Technician Position

Technician Levels	Pay Rate per Cleaning Hour	Incremental Rate Increase	Minimum Months Required to be Eligible for the Next Level
Entry Level Certified Technician	$16.15		3 Months
Intermediate Level Certified Technician	$16.40	$0.25	3 Months
Advanced Level Certified Technician	$16.70	$0.30	3 Months
Master Level Certified Technician	$17.05	$0.35	3 Months
Coach	$17.45	$0.40	4 Months
Advanced Coach	$17.90	$0.45	4 Months
Master Coach	$18.40	$0.50	5 Months

For instance, showcasing success stories of employees who've climbed the ranks within your company can be a powerful recruitment tool. It shows candidates that they're not just stepping into a dead-end job but rather into a role where they can grow. Aligning with what employees seek will make your job offering stand out, whether through clear promotion paths, skill-building programs, or leadership development opportunities.

Meeting Candidate Expectations Through Customization

Some job features are mandatory because they are critical to the role's core responsibilities. However, you can tailor nonessential aspects to meet employee needs, showing that your company values their well-being.

Customization of nonessential requirements and job features is vital to creating appealing job opportunities. Offering competitive pay, flexible work hours, tailored benefits, and clear paths for growth is no longer just an advantage—it's a necessity in today's market.

Pay

Competitive salaries are one of the most critical factors in job design. Employees have a keen sense of what they consider fair, and the best practice is to offer pay that slightly exceeds their expectations, which can give you a competitive edge. Forty-four percent of employees leave jobs due to low income (Caucci, 2021). Benchmarking salaries against industry standards helps you maintain competitive pay and attract top talent to your organization.

Work Hours

Flexibility in scheduling can be precious in industries like retail, hospitality, or any service-based role. Many employees in the service sector juggle multiple responsibilities outside of work, so offering control over their schedules can make your roles stand out. Research shows that over half of employees now prioritize flexible work arrangements, making it a key market offering (*More Than Half*, 2021). Whether it's offering remote options for administrative positions or flexible shifts for front-line staff, adjusting your scheduling can attract candidates who value work–life balance.

A seniority-based system that offers increased flexibility in work hours is highly effective. For example, team members with over two years of service and excellent attendance records can benefit from weekday-only schedules, eliminating weekend hours. This policy rewards both loyalty and performance.

Benefits

You ensure your benefits package aligns with employee needs by tailoring it to match their priorities and preferences. For example, younger employees or college students may value tuition reimbursement. More experienced workers often focus on securing healthcare benefits or planning for retirement to meet their long-term needs. Customizing your benefits to fit the demographics of your team not only increases job appeal but also shows that you're attuned to the unique needs of your workforce.

Growth Opportunities

Highlighting growth opportunities is especially important in the service industry, where many workers see their roles as temporary. Offering clear paths for advancement, performance-based pay increases, or leadership training programs can significantly impact the situation. Employees leave jobs due to a lack of growth opportunities, so demonstrating that there's room to grow within your company is critical for retention.

Incorporating growth opportunities into your recruiting strategy is essential. Clearly outlining pay increases, qualification requirements, and timelines helps candidates see these opportunities as realistic and attainable. This transparency makes applicants feel confident about their potential career progression within the company.

How About the Cost of These Customizations?

The answer is simple: How about the cost of not making your position competitive? In Chapter 1, we calculated the average cost of turnover to be around $18,000. Companies are lowering their costs by making their jobs great instead of suffering from failed hires.

Examples in the Service Industry

The service industry presents unique challenges regarding job design. Still, it also offers opportunities to create roles in which people want to stay.

One major restaurant chain recognized that many of its employees were college students. They introduced a tuition reimbursement program and flexible shifts, allowing students to balance work with their studies. As a result, employee retention increased, and the eatery saw an improvement in employee engagement. This is a perfect example of how customizing job roles to meet the specific needs of your workforce can set your company apart from competitors.

By researching the needs of your workforce and designing jobs that reflect those needs, you make your company a more attractive workplace. Retail, hospitality, and other service industries, where turnover rates tend to run high, see noticeable improvements in attracting and retaining talent when implementing these strategies effectively.

Now that you've created a job attractive to top talent, the next step is to ensure you're hiring suitable candidates. This is where self-veto mechanisms come in—a process that allows candidates to screen themselves out if the job doesn't align with their needs.

Implementing Self-Veto Mechanisms

Recruiting isn't just about finding candidates—it's about ensuring they're committed and capable. Self-veto mechanisms play a critical role here, encouraging candidates to opt out early if the role isn't fit. This proactive approach saves you time and energy by narrowing the applicant pool to those genuinely aligned with the job's requirements. Let's walk through this concept, explore practical examples, and identify the optimal way to use it.

Concept of Self-Veto

Self-veto mechanisms allow applicants to veto their application with their actions: failure to cooperate with a reasonable application process. This mechanism highlights unprofessional or unserious applicants through their actions, ensuring they demonstrate their suitability—or lack thereof—by how they engage in the process. Think of it as a gate-keeping strategy to avoid wasting time on applicants who don't match your expectations. These measures add thoughtful hurdles—like detailed application questions or small post-interview tasks—that test commitment without becoming excessive.

In the service industry, recruiters can focus on quality by filtering out less committed candidates early in the hiring process, ensuring only motivated applicants continue through the stages.

Controlling the Level of Hurdles for Optimal Filtering

Every job demands a different level of scrutiny. For technical or managerial roles, you might need stringent self-veto tools, such as complex assessments. In contrast, positions like customer service or entry-level roles benefit from more accessible hurdles. Statistics show that overly complicated applications put off 60% of candidates, so you must strike the right balance—filter out poor fits without scaring away top talent (Fennell, 2022).

Design these hurdles with care. They need to be perceived as reasonable instead of excessive and nonsensical. Creating an engaging but selective recruitment process helps attract suitable candidates and screen out unsuitable ones.

Examples of Self-Veto Opportunities

Let's explore practical self-veto methods tailored to the service industry.

Detailed Application Forms: Reject the One-Click Application

Comprehensive application forms function as a built-in filter, requiring candidates to put in reasonable and relevant effort. For example, instead of allowing applicants to click once to submit applications on a job board, you can include screening questions about salary expectations, willingness to travel, and physical job requirements. One-click applications attract many unqualified candidates who waste time by submitting their resumes. Still, their genuine interest in the role is often missing. One click is too easy for applicants!

Post-Interview Survey

A post-interview survey shows whether a candidate has follow-through—a crucial trait for roles demanding attention to detail. A survey could include at least one question about the candidate's experience during the interview, what they learned about the company, and how they envision their role. These surveys offer dual benefits in the service industry: They capture candidate perceptions and reveal their willingness to engage in follow-up tasks.

Responsive Communication Checks

You can use communication as a subtle yet effective self-veto mechanism. For instance, sending a follow-up email requesting candidates to complete a small task or provide additional information allows committed candidates to shine. In customer service and hospitality, where responsiveness is a core skill, this step ensures that only those with quick, effective communication continue through the hiring process.

Self-Evaluation Scales

At a later stage in the application process, asking candidates to rate how well the role fits them on a scale of 1 to 10 (with one being wholly unfit and 10 being a perfect match) provides valuable insights. Suppose they fail to respond within a reasonable time. In that case, it acts as a self-veto, while following up with a "why" allows you to gauge their understanding of the role's strengths and weaknesses. Such scales also help you gauge whether candidates have taken the time to understand the job requirements, filtering out those who applied without much thought.

Assignments or Video Reviews

Incorporating assignments or video reviews as part of the recruitment process offers another layer of self-veto. For example, in retail or hospitality roles, you can ask candidates to record a video introducing themselves or describing how they would handle a demanding customer. This approach ensures candidates demonstrate their commitment and essential job skills, such as clear communication and professionalism. Companies employ realistic job previews to give candidates a glimpse into their potential roles and encourage self-selection. These tools ensure that candidates fully understand the job and can decide early on if they are the right fit.

While self-veto mechanisms simplify hiring, you must ensure the process remains manageable. Complex applications frustrate candidates and may drive away even those well-suited. Maintaining a balance between detailed screening and user-friendly steps keeps candidates engaged. Tracking applicant dropout rates at different stages allows you to refine your process and ensure it remains effective over time.

Next, let's explore the concrete benefits of incorporating these mechanisms into your recruitment strategy, from reducing turnover rates to improving overall candidate quality.

Benefits of Self-Veto Mechanisms

In recruitment, self-veto mechanisms streamline hiring, leading candidates to disqualify themselves if they aren't genuinely qualified or interested. Setting deliberate hurdles ensures only committed individuals engage with the process, which saves time and increases the quality of applicants. Let's look at how these mechanisms improve recruitment outcomes with examples from the service industry.

Saving Recruiter Time

The most immediate benefit of self-veto mechanisms is the time saved. Without these filters, recruiters often receive many applications from unqualified or uninterested candidates. For example, retail and hospitality roles tend to attract applicants seeking temporary work, leading to high application volumes and difficulty in identifying the best fit.

Research supports the effectiveness of these strategies. Streamlined processes focusing on high-quality applicants reduce time-to-fill, a crucial advantage in fast-paced industries like retail (Parker, 2023). This approach lightens the workload for HR teams, enabling them to focus on strategic priorities like engaging candidates and strengthening the company's employer brand.

Adjusting Hurdles for Applicant Motivation

Another advantage is the flexibility to adjust hurdle levels. Depending on the position's needs, you can increase or reduce the effort required at different stages. The higher the position level, the more challenging the application hurdle should be. In the early stages of recruitment, a lower hurdle, like a 10-minute application process, works well.

For a home cleaning company, this approach effectively narrows the pool. However, you can increase the hurdle by the final stage when there are about five candidates left. For instance, you might ask the remaining candidates to watch a YouTube video showcasing the company's charitable cleaning efforts for women with cancer. Afterward, they can share their thoughts and any questions. This video review is a reasonable, higher-level hurdle for the final stage.

Shifting Effort to Applicants for Large-Scale Filtering

Self-veto mechanisms are particularly effective when managing large volumes of applications. Retail, house cleaning, commercial cleaning, hospitality, and food service industries often handle hundreds of applications for each open position, especially in high-turnover environments. Requiring candidates to complete pre-employment assessments or technical tests ensures that only those willing to invest time to fulfill a reasonable request remain in the process.

Recruiters save time by shifting a significant portion of the screening responsibility to applicants, forcing applicants to show their qualifications through their actions. Recruiters will do less, observe, and invest time only when the applicants' actions merit it.

Enhancing Overall Recruitment Efficiency and Quality of Applicants

When designed thoughtfully, self-veto mechanisms create a more efficient recruitment process and improve the quality of the candidate pool. Adding extra steps—like assessments or creative application tasks—helps identify individuals who are qualified and genuinely interested in the role. This natural filtering process leaves you with candidates more aligned with your company's needs and values.

Applicants' actions provide a far better indicator of their professionalism and interest level than their words. The self-veto process, rooted in the concept of skin-in-the-game, effectively highlights this by asking candidates to prove their commitment through their actions first.

Service industry companies that apply self-veto mechanisms may improve applicant quality dramatically. This improvement translates to faster hiring cycles and better employee retention, ultimately reducing the costs associated with turnover and new hire training. For example, a retail chain that incorporated pre-employment personality assessments may experience hiring employees who better matched the company culture, resulting in higher employee satisfaction and reduced turnover within the first year.

Recruiters who invest in self-veto strategies also see long-term benefits. Candidates who successfully navigate these hurdles tend to be more engaged during onboarding and perform better on the job. Companies avoid mis-hires by using self-veto mechanisms, which helps them save valuable time and reduce hiring costs over the long term.

Key Takeaways

- Skin-in-the-game recruiting builds in self-veto opportunities for applicants at each stage of the application process.

- Designing a job to enhance its value for specific applicant segments is essential to establishing a solid foundation for the skin-in-the-game recruiting approach.

- Self-veto mechanisms effectively filter out unqualified, not-so-serious, and no longer interested applicants.

- An efficient recruitment process with a self-veto mechanism dramatically reduces time and resource consumption.

While self-veto mechanisms help streamline the process, advocating for your company to attract top talent is equally crucial. Next, let's explore how recruiters can distinguish between effective screening and presenting their organization as the employer of choice.

Chapter 11:

The Fine Balance of Screening and

Advocating

You're sitting in an interview with a bright-eyed candidate who's perfect—on paper and in action. They've got every qualification, but a sense of worry emerges in your mind halfway through. A few questions quickly flash through your mind:

- Is the job good enough for this applicant?

- Is the applicant fully aware of the job's strengths that can genuinely support the applicant's student life?

- How can I elaborate on the job's challenges while letting the applicant's strengths shine so that the applicant is fully prepared to overcome them and grow in the job?

In this chapter, you'll learn how to balance objectivity and advocacy to create a compelling, honest recruiting process that resonates with candidates. You'll discover ways to tailor job messaging to meet applicants' needs, advocating for the job's strengths without overwhelming them. We'll cover how to subtly emphasize benefits, align roles with candidate goals, and avoid the pitfalls of overselling. This balanced approach attracts the right talent and builds trust, ensuring candidates feel understood and valued.

By weaving systematic advocacy into each stage and using data insights, you can enhance candidate engagement and long-term success.

The Dual Role of Recruiters in Service Industries

In the service industry, recruiters play a crucial dual role: They must objectively screen applicants to identify the best fit and authentically advocate for the job and company. Balancing these responsibilities ensures fair hiring while building genuine connections with candidates, fostering long-term engagement, and reducing turnover.

Screening Applicants

As a recruiter, your mission starts with narrowing down the best candidates for the role, which requires objective evaluation. Structured applicant pipelines and interviews ensure fairness by ensuring all applicants receive the same assessment. This method helps you focus on what matters—qualifications, skills, and relevant experience—without getting sidetracked by bias or personal assumptions.

Advocating for the Job Position

The second half of your role revolves around presenting the job—and the company—and how the job can help the applicant and the challenges ahead. Recruitment goes beyond simply filling roles; it involves telling the organization's story genuinely and engagingly. Candidates appreciate transparency, and setting realistic expectations builds trust. This means giving a balanced view—highlighting how the job can help the candidate's goals without glossing over the challenges. For example, candidates who understand a role's perks and difficulties are less likely to leave due to unmet expectations, reducing costly turnover.

A well-executed advocacy strategy also showcases the company's culture and long-term vision. Today's candidates—especially those in the service industry—want to feel connected to a company's values. Highlighting your organization's efforts around diversity and inclusion can make a strong impression. McKinsey reports that companies ranked in the top quartile for racial and ethnic diversity are 35% more likely to achieve higher financial performance, highlighting the clear business advantages of inclusive recruitment practices (*McKinsey Study*, 2015).

Now that you've mastered balancing the roles of screening and advocating, it's time to think about job design. After all, even the best recruitment strategies won't shine without roles tailored to attract the right talent. Let's explore how job design helps you align your offerings with the needs and motivations of your target applicant segments.

Job Design: Being the Best Option for Your Applicant Segments

To attract top talent, recruiters must go beyond generic job listings and design roles that resonate with different segments of applicants. By understanding and addressing each segment's unique needs and preferences, you create compelling job offerings that set your organization apart in a competitive market.

Defining Applicant Segments

Tailoring job offerings starts by categorizing applicants based on their demographic, psychographic, and behavioral traits. Demographic segmentation lays the groundwork for recruitment by identifying experience level, education, and location characteristics.

Psychographic segmentation goes deeper, uncovering applicants' values, attitudes, and motivations. Understanding what drives candidates allows recruiters to align job roles with personal priorities. For instance, a role should emphasize career growth and skill development to attract ambitious candidates while highlighting flexibility to appeal to applicants seeking better work–life balance. This nuanced approach enhances your messaging, creating emotional resonance with potential hires.

Behavioral insights further refine your understanding of applicant preferences. For example, many service industry applicants frequently engage with job postings on social media. Adjusting recruitment strategies based on these behaviors—such as leveraging social media ads—boosts engagement and increases the likelihood of attracting quality candidates.

Recognizing and Addressing Each Segment's Needs and Desires

Once you've segmented applicants, aligning job offerings with their needs becomes essential. Many applicants prioritize working daytime hours and avoiding weekends in the house cleaning industry. To address this, make weekend availability optional, so employees who prefer not to work weekends won't be required to do so. If you can structure roles to meet these expectations, you'll find attracting and retaining top talent easier.

The table below shows what you can do to address the needs and desires of applicants per segment.

Applicants' Segments and Needs

Needs	Applicant Segments					
	No Strong Support	With Direct & Strong Support	Student	Inexperienced and Searching	Professional	Experienced
Hours	Day time hours. No nights. No weekends. No holidays.	Day time hours. No nights. No weekends. No holidays.	Flexible, as long as it supports School	Flexible, as long as it supports work life balance	Flexible, as long as it supports work life balance	Flexible, as long as it supports work life balance
Pay	Need a balance between income and family life	Maximize income	Need a balance between income and available hours to study	Reasonable and stable income	Maximize income	Maximize income
Flexibility	Need more flexible hours	Standard work hours are manageable	Need flexibility to support School	Standard work hours are manageable	Standard work hours are manageable	Standard work hours are manageable
Biggest Desires	Balance income and family needs	Maximize income while still meet family needs	School success, with the financial support from the job.	Reasonable and stable income	Maximize income via growth opportunities	Maximize income via growth opportunities

Meanwhile, career development opportunities appeal to candidates focused on long-term growth. Offering structured training programs or evident career growth can help you engage those motivated by upward mobility. Companies that actively support career development see employees stay longer, leading to higher job satisfaction and reduced turnover rates.

Tracking shifting market trends is essential. Collecting feedback from successful and unsuccessful candidates reveals valuable insights into their changing expectations. Using AI-driven analytics to track these trends enables recruiters to fine-tune job advertisements and value propositions. For example, recruitment platforms increasingly use analytics to identify which roles resonate with different applicant segments, streamlining the hiring process by delivering targeted messages more efficiently.

Now that you understand aligning job offerings with applicant needs, let's move on to the next topic: mapping out job strengths and challenges by segment. This next step will show you how to match candidate expectations with specific job requirements, ensuring fit and satisfaction for long-term success.

Mapping Out Job Strengths and Challenges by Segment

Recruiting for service industry roles requires a strategic approach that considers candidates' specific needs and expectations. From client-facing jobs to behind-the-scenes positions, each role has unique strengths, challenges, and opportunities that recruiters must address thoughtfully to attract top talent effectively.

Client Service Settings

Recruiters in the service industry navigate various client interactions, tailoring their messaging based on whether candidates apply for direct or indirect roles. For customer-facing jobs, you highlight teamwork, customer engagement, and the daily impact these roles have on the organization. In contrast, candidates for behind-the-scenes positions often value communication about how their contributions drive the company's mission. Effective recruiters align their outreach to match these nuances, ensuring candidates connect with opportunities that suit their strengths and priorities.

Pay

Competitive pay remains a crucial factor in attracting talent. Transparency about salary is not just a trend—it's a necessity. Professionals prioritize higher salaries when considering new roles, especially in industries where specific skill sets command a premium. Pay benchmarking ensures your offers stay competitive, reducing turnover risks by satisfying financial expectations early in the process. Moreover, advertising transparent compensation packages reflects fairness and enhances employer branding.

Hours and Flexibility

Daytime and weekday shifts are vital features in many service industry roles. In the home cleaning industry, offering these shifts without weekends appeals to applicants from sectors like retail, food service, security, and caregiving, where evening and weekend work is often required.

Flexible work arrangements have become essential. Many candidates in the service industry seek adaptable schedules, such as hybrid or part-time work, to balance personal responsibilities. A report by Morgan McKinley highlights that more than half of professionals rank flexible work hours among the top benefits they look for (Workers Are Walking Away, 2023). Predictable scheduling allows workers to plan their lives effectively, helping them balance multiple responsibilities while reducing the risk of burnout.

Benefits and Perks

Candidates evaluate roles based on additional perks beyond pay and flexibility. Desirable benefits include health insurance, wellness programs, tuition reimbursements, and work-from-home options. Successful recruiters promote holistic compensation packages, demonstrating that the organization values productivity, employee well-being, and long-term development.

Growth Potential

Career growth opportunities are critical, especially for ambitious candidates. Companies like Google have set benchmarks by offering structured internal mobility and continuous learning initiatives. By providing mentorship programs, training sessions, and leadership development opportunities, your organization is committed to fostering employees' long-term success and growth. This messaging helps attract candidates who value long-term professional growth.

You can create growth opportunities for any job. The seven levels of the cleaning technician role demonstrate that growth is achievable when there are distinct performance levels among employees and when companies are committed to recognizing and rewarding excellent work.

Company Culture and Core Values

It's more important than ever for your organization to communicate its culture and core values actively. Younger candidates, particularly from Gen Z, seek purpose-driven work environments and align themselves with companies that demonstrate social responsibility. Promoting a transparent and inclusive workplace—whether through social media storytelling or employee testimonials—strengthens your employer brand, making attracting and retaining top talent easier.

Job's Challenges and Perceived Weaknesses

Being upfront about a role's challenges builds trust with candidates. Honesty is crucial, but it alone doesn't suffice. When discussing a potential weakness, you should follow up with strategies, outline the available support, and highlight what employees typically learn and feel after overcoming the challenge. Candidates appreciate honesty about the less glamorous aspects of a job, such as dealing with demanding customers or tight deadlines, when recruiters also emphasize the rewards—whether in terms of learning or advancement potential.

Next, let's examine how recruiters can use emotional appeal before shifting to logical persuasion, ensuring candidates feel understood and valued from the first interaction.

Advocating With Emotion First, Then Logic

When recruiting in the service industry, appealing to emotion and logic is crucial for attracting candidates who align with your company's values. Crafting job messaging that connects with the heart and reassures with tangible benefits creates a powerful narrative, making candidates feel inspired and secure in their decisions.

Emotional Appeal

Crafting job messaging that hits the heart and mind can transform your recruitment efforts. Advocacy involves communicating value to job applicants, like the ethical selling process. People make decisions based on emotions and then use logic to justify those choices subconsciously, which means effective advocacy must engage emotionally first to resonate with candidates.

Key Emotional Triggers to Target

When writing emotionally driven job descriptions, aim to tap into triggers like accomplishment, purpose, and status. Emotionally appealing messaging makes potential candidates picture themselves thriving in the role. For instance, rather than saying a restaurant manager will "supervise staff," describe how they'll "lead a passionate team and create memorable customer experiences."

The following emotional hooks are particularly relevant in service industries:

- What will you have? Describe the benefits, job security, and support they'll receive.

- How would you feel? Tap into the pride, satisfaction, and fulfillment they might experience in their work.

- What is the average day like? Outline a typical day, highlighting positive interactions, routine, and variety.

- What is your status as a worker, parent, or student? Address how the role aligns with their identity and personal commitments.

- How do you prove the "good" and defeat the "evil"? Emphasize how their efforts contribute to a cleaner, healthier environment and a happier client base.

See the example of this analysis for a house cleaning company based on their job applicant segments.

Advocacy based on Segments

Advocacy Angles	Applicant Segments					
	No Strong Support	With Direct & Strong Support	Student	Inexperienced and Searching	Professional	Experienced
Have	A steady schedule, reliable income. Take good care of family all evenings and weekends. Growth!	Contribute to family finance substantially, while still, have time to spend with family in evening and weekends.	Great income to pay for school. Flexible schedule, a company that supports your school plans. Have weekends off either to take a class or to do homework.	More and steady income and schedule. The opportunity to grow with the company. Have time for self and family. Have a job that can become a career.	Company with integrity, proud, and support. Have steady schedule and no night. Opportunity to grow within the company.	Flexible schedule, secure job, great working environment, great team members, growth opportunity, and good pay.
Feel	Relieve, in control, happy, fulfil	Happy, pride, accomplished	Happy, relief, focused	Earn more, happier, healthier	Secure, kind, valued	Happy, accomplished, healthier
Average day	Work during the day only. In the evenings and weekends, spend time with family.	Secure income, while get home early and still be able to take care of family in the evening and weekends.	Work in the mornings, go to school in the evenings and weekends. Have plenty of time to do homework in the night or weekends.	Earn more. Work during the day time. Flexibility in the evenings and weekends to focus on personal goals!	Only work during the day, Have a schedule every day. Don't have to drive to the office daily.	Work during the day, have the evenings and nights for the family. Not feeling tired. Can grow to higher level.
Status	Successful, super parent	Provider, equality, and independence	Put together, well on the way to complete school successfully	Successful, accomplish	Professional, valued independent, successful	Healthy, strong, in control, and growth
Good Vs. Evil	Don't have to choose between a good income and take care of family. Who said you can't have both?	Both a key income provider to family and GREAT parent! Who said you can't do both?	Don't have to be broke to finish school. Not having to pick between an education and being able to support for self (independence)	Be Successful with an enjoyable job that you can earn more, grow and become happier. Who said you can not have a enjoyable physical job, earn great money, grow professionally, and a career? You can have all three!	You are good at cleaning and you love it. Who said cleaning can not be a respected career? Cleaning is not just a job but could be an amazing career.	Achieve an healthy job and a well paid career. Have both!

133

This approach communicates practical job details and builds an emotional connection by framing their role as meaningful and rewarding.

Following With Logic

While emotions capture attention, logic ensures candidates trust what you're offering. Data-driven elements, like transparent salary details, healthcare coverage, or career advancement programs, reassure applicants that your promises aren't just empty words. For example, you should highlight career growth paths and mentorship programs. It appeals to candidates, especially millennials. They will be 75% of the workforce by 2025 (Fry, 2018).

In service industries, where candidates might worry about burnout or job instability, logical elements are essential to balance emotional messaging. A candidate considering a customer service role might find the promise of making a difference appealing. Still, they must also know that the company provides practical support like health insurance and vacation days.

Emotional engagement and logical reassurance create job messaging that captivates and builds trust. For instance, describing how a hotel concierge can "create unforgettable guest experiences" becomes even more compelling when paired with details about training programs and career progression. Blending these elements ensures candidates feel inspired by the possibilities and confident in the company's ability to deliver.

Now that we've explored the art of crafting balanced job messaging, let's move on to the broader challenge of maintaining equilibrium—knowing when to engage emotionally and focus on facts. Recruiters must strike the right balance, where managing dual roles becomes crucial to their success.

The Key Is Balance: Not Too Much, Not Too Little

When recruiting in service industries, finding the balance between promoting a role and managing expectations is essential. Overselling a job may excite candidates, but it can backfire if the role doesn't meet their expectations. On the flip side, underpromoting leaves candidates uninspired, missing the chance to connect emotionally with what could be a perfect fit.

The Risk of Overadvocating

Advocating too hard can overwhelm candidates, making them feel that someone is selling them on the role rather than welcoming them into a potential partnership. This reaction, known as the "reactance" effect in psychology, happens when people sense excessive influence on their choices, often leading them to resist or withdraw. Imagine being on a first date where the other person constantly talks about their best qualities—chances are, you'd lose interest or feel uncomfortable. The same goes for recruiting; excessive advocacy can come across as pushy and turn candidates away.

Overselling can lead to unmet expectations, which is a significant contributor to high turnover. Turnover costs in hospitality and retail industries can result in lost productivity and recruitment expenses. Building trust through accurate messaging is crucial to retention. Candidates might become skeptical if a job ad sounds too good to be true, assuming hidden issues in the workplace. This skepticism can deter top talent from applying in the first place, especially as millennials and Gen Z demand authenticity and transparency from employers.

For example, portraying a customer service role as stress-free misleads candidates. When reality hits—dealing with demanding customers or long shifts—disappointment follows, often driving employees to leave within their first six months.

We should openly share that the job can be stressful, especially when dealing with challenging customers. However, our training program effectively equips associates to manage these situations, and many have become experts through practice and support. While it's not easy, with dedication and a strong team, they have excelled in handling work-related stress.

The Risk of Underadvocating

Consider a scenario where a restaurant recruiter mentions only the pay and shift schedule but omits the camaraderie and professional development opportunities the role offers. Candidates may pass up the opportunity, perceiving it as just another job with little room for growth. In service industries with high competition for talent, this kind of underadvocating leaves businesses struggling to attract the right people.

Striking the Right Balance

To balance emotional appeal with accurate information, recruiters should start with storytelling. Describe how a role fits into the broader picture—creating memorable guest experiences or becoming a valued team member. Then, follow with factual details like pay, benefits, and flexibility. Workers increasingly prioritize work–life balance and access to career development, so highlighting these aspects appeals to both the heart and mind.

Recruiters in service industries must disclose job challenges and solutions. Discussing a position's perceived weaknesses is as crucial as advocating its strengths. Retaining employees goes beyond hiring the right fit; it requires keeping them engaged and helping them overcome challenges ahead. Hence, disclosure of both these challenges and the training and support to overcome them is vital.

Now that you've explored how to strike this balance, let's move on to the next step: integrating advocacy throughout the recruitment process to sustain candidate engagement and reduce turnover.

Integrating Advocacy Into the Recruitment Process

Incorporating advocacy into each stage of the recruitment process enhances employer branding, builds trust, and attracts better-suited candidates. Employee advocacy programs significantly improve recruitment outcomes, leading to more substantial retention rates and deeper engagement between employees and employers.

Job Ads

To create compelling job ads

1. Use messaging that appeals both emotionally and logically.

2. Describe life in the role by sharing concrete scenarios candidates can relate to.

3. Be transparent about the challenges candidates may face and the solutions to succeed.

This honesty resonates with potential applicants and builds credibility. For example, if you're hiring for a restaurant manager, describe the thrill of leading a dynamic team, the pressures of maintaining service standards during peak hours, and your training program of "4 Steps to Win the Peak Hour Game!" Messaging that combines emotion with logic attracts more candidates and reduces early turnover due to unmet expectations.

Employee Testimonial Videos

Candidates trust firsthand employee stories more than corporate statements. Share employee testimonials to offer genuine insights into what it's like to work at your organization. Videos showing employees discussing challenges and personal growth in the company can connect emotionally with viewers. Employee stories influence many candidates' application decisions, mainly when they reflect day-to-day experiences or career progressions. Showcasing diverse employees in these videos also broadens your appeal to various talent segments.

Interview Questions Designed for Advocacy

The interview process offers an excellent opportunity to advocate for the position while assessing fit. Craft questions that allow candidates to reflect on the role's emotional and practical aspects. For example, you might ask, "How will this job improve your life if we hire you?" This type of question encourages candidates to reflect on the job's advantages, demonstrating strong advocacy that is both assertive and tailored to the situation.

Job Details and Brochures

Create job descriptions and brochures by blending emotional appeal with precise, factual details. This approach ensures candidates feel connected to the role and well-informed about practical benefits. Include visuals and stories that illustrate the impact employees make. Service industry candidates, for example, value flexibility and professional development. Therefore, complementing messages about purpose with information about mentorship programs and healthcare benefits can build trust and clarity.

Job Interviews

Incorporate advocacy naturally into interviews by weaving stories about company culture and employee achievements. Address both emotional concerns—like job satisfaction—and practical ones, such as salary and benefits. This conversational style builds rapport and shows that you care about candidates' well-being and professional growth.

News Media Interviews or Publications

Boost advocacy efforts by sharing employee success stories through press releases or interviews. Organizations like Cisco and Coca-Cola have successfully amplified their employer brand by featuring employee advocates on platforms like LinkedIn. Such visibility helps candidates understand the organization's mission and values, strengthening their attraction to the company.

Company Events, Photos, or Videos

Using multimedia content to highlight your company's culture fosters emotional connections with potential candidates. Photos and videos from company events featuring employees from diverse backgrounds demonstrate inclusivity and teamwork. This personal touch makes the company more relatable and appealing to applicants, especially in industries where teamwork is critical to success.

Incorporating advocacy throughout the recruitment process requires intentional strategies, but the benefits are clear. A well-executed advocacy program strengthens your employer brand, increases job satisfaction, and reduces turnover—critical factors in industries with high churn rates. Organizations with vital employee advocacy programs retain talent and experience better alignment with employee expectations.

By embedding advocacy into every interaction with candidates, you attract top talent and set the foundation for long-term employee engagement. Now, let's shift gears to explore the art of balance—how to engage candidates effectively without overwhelming them or overselling the role.

Key Takeaways

- Service industry recruiters have roles in screening applicants and advocating for the job.

- Defining applicant segments and understanding their needs is critical for targeted job design.

- Openly sharing a job's challenges and strategies to address them is as essential as highlighting its strengths.

- Leading with emotion and backing up with logic creates a compelling narrative.

- Overadvocating can be detrimental. It is vital also to disclose the position's challenges and how to overcome them. Advocacy should be honest, natural, and contextual to foster trust.

- Advocacy should be integral to the recruitment process to achieve the best results.

Effective recruitment is not just about advocacy—it's also about making more intelligent decisions backed by data. With industries shifting toward predictive hiring, recruiters must move from relying solely on intuition to leveraging analytics. Let's explore how harnessing data insights helps optimize strategies, ensuring every hire is a well-informed decision.

Chapter 12:

Harnessing Data Insights—From Intuition to Informed Decisions

Picture this: You're sitting in an interview, nodding as a candidate describes their work history. Something about them feels right—the confident handshake, the wonderful smile, the well-timed jokes. So, you trust your gut and hire them on the spot. Fast-forward three months: They've ghosted a client and misfiled essential documents. Now, HR is forwarding resignation letters from their whole team to you. Oops. It turns out that a great handshake and a wonderful smile didn't predict performance at all.

This chapter explores how data insights can transform your recruitment process, enabling faster, more objective decisions that promote diversity and reduce bias. You'll learn to quantify all recruitment data—interview responses, surveys, and application details—and use predictive analytics to identify candidates most likely to succeed. Discover how tools like ATS and AI streamline evaluations, improve job–candidate matching, and enhance recruitment efficiency. You can refine hiring strategies and reduce turnover by analyzing recruitment patterns and implementing key metrics.

The Limitations of Intuition in Recruitment

Intuition plays a role in hiring, but relying on it alone can introduce biases and lead to inconsistent outcomes. Dr. Kahneman's research shows how structured methods, combined with data-driven insights, provide a more reliable framework for recruitment—utilizing human judgment and informed intuition based on objective analysis for profoundly better hiring decisions in the long run (Cynkar, 2007).

Intuition vs. Data

Should You Trust Your Gut?

We start with the data. But the final call is always gut. It's informed intuition.
~ Reed Hastings, CEO, Netflix ~

Dr. Kahneman's Insights

Dr. Kahneman has shown that relying solely on intuition often leads to inconsistent decisions. His research, rooted in behavioral economics, divides thinking into two modes: fast, intuitive judgments (System 1) and deliberate, analytical reasoning (System 2) (Loo, 2021). Intuitive decisions may feel right in the moment, but they often lack the accuracy and objectivity that careful analysis provides.

Kahneman's collaboration with the Israeli military highlighted how unstructured interviews—based purely on intuition—led to inconsistent outcomes (Cynkar, 2007). His push toward structured interviews laid the groundwork for modern hiring practices, showing that objective methods significantly improve the accuracy of placements and reduce hiring mistakes.

Understanding Cognitive Biases

Cognitive biases creep into hiring decisions without you even realizing it, clouding your judgment. Kahneman's research points out that overconfidence bias is especially problematic—recruiters often believe they can spot the perfect candidate by instinct alone. This overconfidence creates a false sense of security, making you less likely to rely on data that could uncover hidden insights.

In the service industry, hiring teams often prioritize personality and customer-facing skills. Still, this approach can backfire by causing high turnover and misaligned hires. Over time, it becomes clear that purely intuitive decisions introduce unpredictability and risk into your hiring strategy.

Halo Effect: Another Prominent Bias in Recruiting

You must stay aware of the halo effect, as it can become a cognitive trap. This bias happens when one positive trait—like a confident communication style or charismatic presence—automatically leads you to assume other positive characteristics, such as confidence, honesty, being a great problem-solver, or being a great team player. It's easy to fall into this trap, especially in service industries, where personality is more important than job competence.

Imagine hiring someone because they seemed friendly and confident during an interview, only to realize later that they lack critical skills for the role. Kahneman's work explains that while traits like charisma are admirable to have, focusing too heavily on them can cause you to miss red flags and lead to costly mismatches between hires and roles.

Structured Interview

Structured interviews buffer against these biases, providing a standardized framework that ensures fairness and consistency. With this approach, every candidate answers the same question in the same order and with the same scoring criteria, allowing you to compare them objectively. By sticking to predefined questions, you're keeping things fair and collecting measurable data that helps refine future hiring strategies.

Kahneman found that the Israeli military significantly improved the accuracy of soldier placements by using structured interviews (Cynkar, 2007). This showed how structured methods can align individual strengths with role requirements, setting a precedent for evidence-based hiring.

Structured interviews hold significant value in the service industry, as hiring managers often handle large volumes of applicants. Instead of relying on gut feelings, you can use structured assessments to evaluate critical competencies systematically and comparably, like communication skills or problem-solving abilities. This ensures that decisions are based on objective data rather than fleeting impressions, leading to better hires and reduced turnover.

Intuition: Improve With Data Insights

Intuition isn't off the table—Kahneman suggests you treat it as the final step rather than the primary driver. You build a solid foundation for decision-making by gathering and analyzing data first while intentionally withholding judgment. You can only reflect on your gut feelings to see if they align with the evidence. For instance, after rating candidates on relevant attributes, you might consider your instinct about their cultural fit.

This hybrid approach lets intuition refine the decision without overshadowing the data, adding depth without sacrificing objectivity.

Informed Intuition is essential for making well-rounded hiring decisions. Combining humility, data, and thoughtful intuition will improve your accuracy and fairness in selecting candidates. Here's how to approach this method:

- **Humility of the recruiter:** Start by recognizing that biases can cloud even the most experienced judgment—approach every hiring decision with humility, acknowledging that intuition alone can lead to errors. Stay open to new insights and avoid letting your ego guide your choices.

- **Delay judgment:** Before making any conclusions, focus on gathering accurate data and taking time to review it. By pausing and grounding yourself in concrete information, you prevent snap judgments and get a more precise, objective view of each candidate.

- **Embrace intuition post-data review:** After examining the data and understanding the insights, allow your intuition to guide you. This informed intuition isn't based only on gut feelings but draws from your gathered context. It gives you a balanced, insightful perspective for making final decisions.

With these steps, you're not abandoning intuition but refining it. This process helps reduce biases, improve fairness, and leads to better, more reliable hiring outcomes.

This method works particularly well in service industries, where hard and soft skills are critical. Say you're hiring for a front-desk position at a hotel. You've rated candidates based on experience and technical skills. Still, your gut tells you one candidate has a certain warmth that fits your brand.

You resist the urge to judge too early, completing the structured interview and scoring strictly according to the criteria. After reviewing the entire application results, you notice that, despite the candidate's warmth, they scored low in both physicality and coachability—skills essential for the role. Your intuition shifts from initial optimism to serious concern, leading you to decide not to proceed with this candidate.

Using data to guide the decision ensures you don't miss essential qualifications, while intuition helps fine-tune the final choice.

Humility

Humility is essential when it comes to improving hiring practices. Kahneman argues that recognizing the limits of your intuition is the first step toward sound decision-making. It takes humility to admit that structured methods may outperform instinct. Still, this openness makes you a better recruiter based on the recruiting results instead of individual ego or pride. Service industries that embrace structured approaches—while staying open to refining their methods based on outcomes—are better positioned to reduce turnover, improve employee alignment, and build resilient teams.

This mindset creates space for continuous learning. When hiring decisions are tracked and analyzed over time, you can identify patterns and adjust your approach accordingly. For example, if data shows that specific interview questions consistently predict performance, you can integrate those questions into future interviews. At the same time, if your instincts have steered you wrong in the past, you learn to recalibrate your intuition based on those experiences. This ongoing learning cycle ensures that your recruitment practices evolve and adapt, setting the foundation for long-term success.

You've seen how data and data insights can refine intuition, but what's next? It's time to harness the power of data to build a recruitment pipeline that's efficient, equitable, and predictive of long-term success. Let's dive into how you can integrate data-driven practices to transform your hiring process.

Building a Data-Driven Recruitment Pipeline

Building a data-driven recruitment pipeline requires a strategic blend of defined qualifications, thoughtful assessments, and structured processes. By aligning your recruitment practices with data insights, you create a system that identifies top talent and supports long-term retention, even in fast-paced service industries where turnover can be challenging.

Defining Critical Qualification Attributes

When building a data-driven recruitment pipeline in the fast-paced service industry, defining the essential qualifications is where it all begins. It's the first step in merging intuition with data insights. As an HR leader, recruiter, business owner, or HR technology innovator, you know that nailing down these qualifications is crucial. Without a clear understanding of what skills and traits your ideal candidate should have, the recruitment process becomes guesswork.

In industries like retail, you focus on delivering excellent customer service because you constantly interact with customers. A candidate's ability to communicate effectively, handle difficult situations gracefully, and provide customers with a positive experience would be nonnegotiable. In the healthcare industry, you likely prioritize empathy, attention to detail, and the ability to perform well under pressure.

Defining these key attributes creates a roadmap for your recruitment strategy. Each role has unique demands, and aligning your recruitment efforts with your organization's needs ensures that every hire adds value. It's like drafting a blueprint for a house—without a solid plan, you risk building something unstable that won't last. Clear and detailed qualification attributes form the foundation of a robust recruitment process.

Developing Assessment Tools

Once you've established the qualifications for each role, the next step is to develop practical assessment tools to measure applicants' competence scores on each qualification requirement. This isn't just about throwing in generic personality tests or asking candidates to solve brain-teasers—the tools you create or choose need to measure job-related competencies that matter to your business. For instance, if you're hiring for a customer service position in hospitality, you might develop a scenario-based test that simulates a typical guest interaction. How a candidate handles a demanding guest would give you insights into their conflict-resolution skills and EQ, which are vital in this field.

Interviews are another essential tool to assess an applicant's competencies, allowing you to evaluate their qualifications in real time. During interviews, you can dive deeper into their experiences and problem-solving abilities while gauging their communication style and cultural fit. A well-structured interview should include behavioral questions that prompt candidates to share how they've handled similar situations. This method, known as behavioral interviewing, helps you predict future performance based on past behavior. Asking open-ended questions like, "Tell me about a time when you had to manage a difficult customer," can reveal critical insights about their soft skills, adaptability, and EQ.

Various recruitment tools help you evaluate candidates thoroughly, including reviewing application information, resumes, surveys, and assessments. Each element adds valuable insights. Application information gives a snapshot of the candidate's background, while the resume highlights their skills, experience, and relevant achievements. Surveys and assessments dig deeper, revealing personality traits, strengths, and areas for growth—vital for roles requiring specific attributes or skills. These tools work together, providing a complete view of each applicant so you can make more informed, objective hiring decisions and find the best fit for your team and company culture.

Cognitive ability tests are another excellent tool for assessing problem-solving capabilities, especially for roles that require quick thinking under pressure. For example, an airline customer service rep must make fast, informed decisions when handling delays or overbooked flights. Using tools that assess these skills helps ensure you're hiring someone who can excel, not just someone who interviews well.

Implementing a Consistent Scoring System

Imagine entering a cooking competition where judges score contestants based on different criteria. One judge loves presentation, while another only cares about flavor. The result? Chaos. The same goes for recruitment—if different hiring managers evaluate candidates with inconsistent criteria, the process becomes subjective and unreliable.

A consistent scoring system ensures fairness for all candidates. Scoring applicants against predefined metrics ensures you assess each candidate somewhat based on their performance and suitability for the role. This standardization is critical in eliminating personal biases, allowing merit to take center stage. For example, a hiring manager might prefer a candidate who graduated from the same alma mater. At the same time, another might focus more on how well the candidate performed in a practical test. A consistent scoring system ensures that both managers use the same criteria to evaluate candidates.

When you have a lot of candidates to sift through, as is often the case in service industries, using a consistent scoring system makes it easier to compare applicants side by side. You're not just picking someone who "feels right," but someone who has demonstrated their qualifications compared to other candidates.

Designing the Recruitment Process With Self-Veto Options

One clever approach to assess candidate engagement in recruitment is through self-veto options. This method relies on candidates' actions, or lack thereof, to signal their interest and suitability for the role.

Establishing these small but meaningful checkpoints allows candidates to demonstrate their genuine investment in the role. For example, suppose a candidate ignores a simple request to provide feedback on a 30-second video. In that case, it's likely a sign they're either disinterested or unwilling to put in the effort, signaling to you, "I'm not worth your time." This way, you avoid moving forward with candidates who aren't serious without confrontation or lengthy deliberation. It helps you focus on those who demonstrate they're a strong fit through their willingness to engage fully.

Now that you've seen how self-veto options can simplify weeding out disengaged candidates, it's equally important to maintain consistency in the next steps of your process. Let's look at how structured interviews and thorough documentation can further improve your recruitment outcomes.

Structured Interviews and Documentation

Structured interviews and consistent data recording have become essential to modern recruitment strategies. By standardizing the interview process and leveraging data-driven insights, organizations reduce bias, enhance diversity, and ensure fair hiring practices—ultimately building more robust, more effective teams.

Conducting Structured Interviews

In today's fast-moving recruitment environment, structured interviews have become essential for making fair and informed hiring decisions. They go beyond rigid question sets to promote consistency and accuracy across all candidate evaluations. When every applicant answers the same set of job-relevant questions, you eliminate guesswork, reduce bias, and enhance decision-making quality. Google found that adopting structured interviews improved interviewers' preparedness and saved 40 minutes per interview—no small feat when hiring at scale (Millet, 2023).

This method keeps you focused on what matters—evaluating competencies that align with the role rather than relying on intuition or "gut feelings," which often introduce unconscious bias.

It's Possible to Quantify All Recruiting Data

Can stress levels be quantified? The answer is yes. A scale from 1 to 7 can measure stress. 1 means no stress. 7 means so stressful that one can barely function. To establish more consistent measures, we can define 4 as average—the normal state of life with a mixture of tension and peace. We can go further to define 5 as more than the average level of stress and 6 as very stressful. No measurement is perfect. But, if we measure consistently, the change of these scores from one applicant to another can tell a powerful story.

We should quantify recruiting data as much as we can. Consistency in scoring criteria is the key.

Enhancing the Candidate Experience

A structured and transparent interview process ensures candidates leave a positive impression of your company. By nature, people perceive a structured interview process to be well organized. This led to an optimistic projection of good management of the company. Asking every applicant the same questions and evaluating them using consistent criteria builds trust and reassurance. This sense of fairness improves the candidate experience, crucial in shaping your employer brand. When candidates have a positive recruitment experience, they feel motivated to apply again in the future, even if they didn't get hired the first time.

When you respect and value candidates, they're more likely to share positive experiences with others, strengthening your company's reputation as an employer of choice. This goodwill goes a long way, especially in competitive job markets where every touchpoint matters.

Consistent Data Recording

Structured interviews only work well if paired with consistent data recording. When you don't document interview responses systematically, you lose valuable insights, and comparing candidates becomes challenging. When you record data consistently, you ensure it's available for analysis, allowing you to make data-driven hiring decisions. For instance, spotting recurring skill gaps across candidates can help you tweak job descriptions or improve your talent-sourcing strategies.

Using Technology for Better Documentation

ATSs make consistent data recording much more manageable. A well-organized ATS can manage candidates from application to onboarding, clearly showing where improvements are needed. These systems allow recruiters to track outcomes, identifying which interview questions and assessment methods best predict job success. Over time, this data becomes a valuable resource, allowing you to improve your recruitment strategies continuously.

Imagine that candidates who excel in specific problem-solving exercises perform better in customer service roles. You can then adjust your interview focus to prioritize those areas, ensuring you hire individuals who thrive in the role. Over time, refining these processes saves both time and resources while boosting hiring success.

Legal Compliance and Risk Management

Consistent documentation isn't just about making better hiring decisions—it also reduces legal risks. The evaluation of every candidate focused on job-relevant criteria, ensuring compliance with equal employment opportunity laws. This is especially important in high-volume hiring industries, such as hospitality and retail, as subjective judgments can unintentionally slip into the process.

Maintaining thorough records protects your organization from discrimination claims and demonstrates a commitment to fair hiring practices. This proactive approach helps minimize legal risks and builds trust with candidates and employees.

Improving Long-Term Hiring Outcomes

Consistent documentation also validates your hiring strategies over time. By tracking employee performance after they join, you can assess how well your interview process predicted their success. This loop helps you refine your recruitment strategies by analyzing real-world outcomes. For example, if employees hired through structured interviews consistently outperform those hired through unstructured methods, you have solid evidence to continue using that approach.

Conversely, identifying ineffective assessments helps you eliminate time-wasting elements from the process. This ensures that recruiters and candidates benefit from a streamlined, efficient system.

While structured interviews and consistent data recording lay the foundation for better hiring, data analytics takes things to the next level. When organizations analyze their information, they uncover insights that drive continuous improvement. Next, let's look at how applying data analytics can refine your recruitment strategies and help you select the best talent for the job.

Applying Data Analytics

Recruitment decisions based solely on intuition often lead to inconsistent results. Still, data analytics offers a more innovative, more strategic alternative. By leveraging techniques like exploratory data analysis, predictive models, and AI tools, recruiters can uncover hidden patterns, streamline processes, and improve candidate fit and long-term retention.

Exploratory Data Analysis

You start with exploratory data analysis (EDA) to move from intuition to informed recruitment decisions. EDA helps you uncover patterns and trends by evaluating historical hiring data. In the service industry, EDA can reveal which job boards yield the most long-term employees or how specific roles attract candidates with high retention rates. This analysis allows you to fine-tune your recruitment strategy by focusing on the best sources for high-quality talent, ultimately improving efficiency and candidate fit.

For instance, companies have employed EDA to identify specific competencies that correlate with success in customer service roles, helping them proactively build candidate pipelines and improve new hire quality.

Descriptive Data Analysis

Once you've explored your data, descriptive analytics helps you quantify relationships and establish benchmarks. This means understanding how factors like experience or education relate to recruitment performance. Descriptive analytics is especially valuable for setting fair and standardized evaluation criteria. For example, a recruiter can compare how candidates with varying degrees or backgrounds perform within the first year, ensuring an objective and consistent process.

With descriptive metrics, you not only enhance fairness but also eliminate inefficiencies. Companies that adopt structured data models, like those used by Unilever, significantly reduce their time-to-hire from four months to just two weeks by automating evaluations and scoring candidates systematically.

Predictive Data Analysis

Predictive analytics helps you forecast recruitment outcomes by analyzing historical data. This is where data-driven strategies shine. You can build models that predict whether a candidate will thrive in your workplace or determine the likelihood of employee turnover. Tools like IBM's Watson Recruitment use predictive analytics to match candidates to job requirements and company culture, improving retention rates significantly. EmployJoy.ai developed the first hire-or-not-hire AI recommendation model for the service industry, which reduced the turnover rate by 50%.

Predictive analytics is crucial when companies make rapid decisions in competitive job markets. For example, forecasting which positions will become critical allows you to create ready talent pools and reduce last-minute hiring stress.

Regression Analysis

Regression analysis refines predictions by showing how strongly variables relate to one another. This technique helps you determine which candidate attributes—such as problem-solving skills or interpersonal abilities—most strongly predict job performance. In the service industry, where soft skills are paramount, regression models can offer recruiters a more nuanced understanding of success predictors, enabling targeted hiring strategies.

For instance, when evaluating candidates for customer-facing roles, regression analysis might highlight that interpersonal skills are a stronger predictor of success than prior industry experience, guiding recruiters to prioritize these traits during the selection process.

Machine Learning and AI

Integrating machine learning and AI into your recruitment process empowers you to enhance data-driven strategies. These technologies analyze large volumes of candidate data, automate repetitive tasks, and identify subtle patterns that might escape human attention. AI-powered ATSs help streamline recruitment by ranking candidates, sending automated follow-ups, and providing real-time hiring analytics.

Case studies show that companies using AI enjoy dramatic efficiency gains. IBM, for example, reduced candidate screening times by 75%, while Unilever enhanced employee performance and retention through AI-driven assessments (Ayade, 2024). With AI chatbots and natural language processing tools, recruiters can engage candidates quickly, offering personalized interactions while collecting valuable data for further analysis.

Blending AI with human insight reduces bias and improves decision-making quality. However, human intuition still enhances recruiting decision quality, but only after all data are collected independently to minimize bias and only after these data are reviewed and analyzed. Only then does human intuition add the most value. To make this work, recruiters must forcefully and intentionally delay judgment until all data are reviewed and analyzed.

Incorporating these data analytics techniques into recruitment helps you create strategies tailored to your needs while reducing turnover and improving hire quality. The next step? Understand the limitations of intuition in recruitment because relying on a handshake or gut feeling alone no longer works.

Key Takeaways

- Recruiting based on intuition alone is dangerous. Intuition is vital in recruiting only after reviewing data and understanding its insights.

- Structured processes and consistent scoring improve objectivity.

- Analytics can significantly increase recruitment success rates.

Even with the best data-driven strategies, noise and bias can influence recruitment decisions. Minor inconsistencies in evaluations or unconscious preferences may sneak in, impacting outcomes. Next, we'll explore decision hygiene, a framework designed to minimize these biases and ensure fair and consistent hiring decisions.

Chapter 13:

Decision Hygiene—Minimizing

Noise and Bias in Recruitment

You're reviewing candidates for a sales role, and fatigue kicks in after an hour of interviews. Without realizing it, you start favoring applicants who remind you of someone familiar—like that charming college friend you trust. A qualified candidate with fewer "relatable" vibes slips through the cracks. By the end of the day, you're second-guessing yourself: Did you pick the best person or just the one that felt easy? See, even the sharpest recruiters aren't immune to noise and bias.

This chapter guides you through methods to reduce bias and noise in hiring, helping you make more objective, effective decisions that benefit your team and the company. You'll learn to create a fair hiring process using structured interviews, blind hiring techniques, and standardized screening. You can build a diverse, high-performing workforce by recognizing and addressing unconscious biases, applying consistent criteria, and focusing on skills and qualifications.

These approaches ensure each candidate has an equal opportunity, enhancing team quality, lowering turnover, and supporting a more inclusive workplace.

The Concept of Decision Hygiene

Decision hygiene in recruitment focuses on refining the decision-making process to minimize bias and inconsistency, ensuring fairer and more reliable hiring outcomes. Balancing human insight with structured frameworks promotes objective evaluations based on skills and qualifications rather than subjective impressions or fluctuating external factors leading to wrong hires.

Understanding Decision Hygiene

A well-known example is how service industry recruiters often lean toward candidates with "good cultural fit," which can become code for selecting those with similar backgrounds. Decision hygiene helps counter this tendency by clearly measuring qualification and recruiting pipelines that strip away subjective preferences.

This approach leads to better hiring decisions, fewer training failures, significantly reduced turnover, lower recruitment and training costs, increased profitability, and a more enjoyable workplace environment.

Bias and Noise: What Are the Differences?

Bias and noise are distinct but equally disruptive. Bias introduces systematic error—predictably skewing decisions in one direction. For example, hiring managers may favor applicants with similar interests or backgrounds, reinforcing stereotypes and narrowing workforce diversity and the team's capacity and performance.

Noise, by contrast, involves random and inconsistent misjudgment. Imagine two recruiters evaluating the same candidate under different conditions: one on a busy Monday morning and the other on a calm Friday afternoon. Their assessments may vary widely, not because of the candidate's merit but due to fluctuating external factors such as mood, time, or fatigue. This variability can be especially problematic in fast-paced industries like hospitality, where multiple hiring managers interact with candidates across different shifts.

The illustration below describes noise and bias, and an accurate hiring decision.

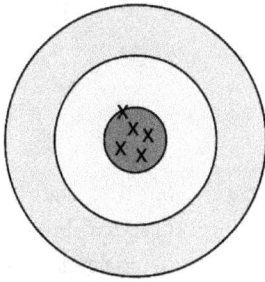

Accurate

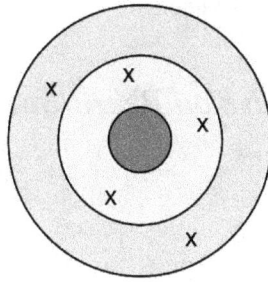

Noisy

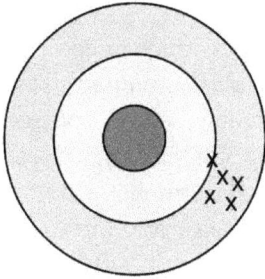

Biased

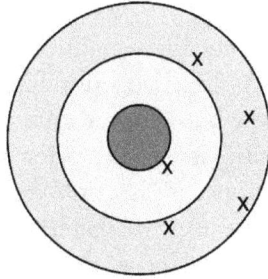

Biased & Noisy

Impact of Bias on Recruitment

Unchecked bias can significantly skew hiring outcomes, leading to homogeneous workplaces, underperforming team members, and perpetuating inequalities. Affinity bias—the tendency to favor those with shared characteristics—can undermine objective hiring. This bias may limit an organization's potential in the service industry, where workforce diversity boosts business performance.

Recruiting bias can mislead you into poor hiring decisions, leading to disastrous outcomes for new hires. For example, many recruiters have experienced a promising new hire who fails unexpectedly early on. They start with high expectations, fully convinced the candidate is a perfect fit. But as soon as training begins, disappointment hits—the new hire is struggling! This often stems from unconscious bias, leading the recruiter to a misplaced sense of confidence in the candidate.

Impact of Noise on Recruitment

Noise disrupts consistency and reduces the reliability of hiring decisions. Recruiters in fast-paced industries like retail or hospitality often find it challenging to maintain uniform standards during interviews. For instance, one hiring manager might rate a candidate more leniently because of a positive mood. At the same time, another could judge more harshly after dealing with a difficult client.

The result? Two equally qualified candidates may receive vastly different evaluations based on unrelated factors. Kahneman's research emphasizes that while biases are predictable, noise introduces randomness, making it even harder to pinpoint and fix (Nesterak, 2021). Reducing noise is essential for fair recruitment, especially in large teams where multiple managers assess the same applicants.

Standardized tools like scoring rubrics or interview templates help curb noise, ensuring evaluators assess every candidate consistently. Blind recruitment methods, which remove identifying information from applications, are another effective strategy for minimizing bias and noise.

Consistent and objective recruitment practices promote fairness and improve workforce quality. Organizations implementing decision hygiene strategies attract a broader talent pool, creating innovative and adaptive teams. While intuition still plays a role in hiring, decision hygiene ensures gut feelings don't dominate the process, striking a balance between human insight and structured data-driven evaluation.

Now that we've covered how decision hygiene works, let's shift gears. Implementing structured interviews is the next logical step in building more reliable hiring frameworks. This practice helps align all stakeholders, ensuring everyone evaluates candidates through the same lens. Let's take a closer look at how structured interviews can revolutionize your recruitment strategy.

Implementing Structured Interviews

Implementing structured interviews ensures a fair, consistent, and objective hiring process by evaluating every candidate based on the same set of job-relevant criteria. This method improves the accuracy of candidate assessments and strengthens legal compliance, making it extremely valuable for service industry recruitment.

Consistency in Questions and Order

This approach removes the risk of assessing candidates based on different criteria, creating equal opportunities regardless of background, personality, or first impressions.

For example, imagine that you hire for a customer service role and ask one candidate about handling angry customers. In contrast, someone asks another about their favorite work experience. It becomes nearly impossible to compare their answers fairly. Structured interviews prevent this by maintaining a consistent approach and ensuring that evaluators consistently assess every candidate based on the same relevant skills.

Facilitating Objective Comparisons

Structured interviews allow you to compare candidates objectively. Something powerful happens when recruiters consistently ask the same questions in the same order and use identical scoring criteria. They can observe and evaluate a candidate's responses with heightened accuracy and objectivity. The more they repeat this process, the more reliable and objective their assessments become.

Structured interviews can predict job performance up to twice as effectively as unstructured ones (Zojceska, 2019). This holds particular value in the service industry, where consistent performance in roles like customer service or sales is essential. Directly asking the same questions lets you compare candidates' responses, ensuring fair and accurate evaluations.

More Predictive

Structured interviews are also more predictive of future job performance. Unlike unstructured interviews, which often rely on intuition and informal conversations, structured interviews focus on questions to measure critical competencies relevant to the role. These questions, frequently based on techniques like STAR (Situation, Task, Action, Result), allow you to gauge how candidates have handled specific situations in the past, giving you a clearer picture of how they might perform in the future.

Structured interviews offer higher predictive validity, meaning they are more likely to identify candidates who will succeed.

More Legally Compliant

Structured interviews offer a clear advantage by helping companies maintain legal compliance. Evaluating all candidates using consistent criteria minimizes the risk of bias or discrimination claims. This becomes especially crucial in the service industry, where high turnover increases the chances of legal disputes. By documenting that every candidate was assessed fairly, structured interviews provide solid evidence to defend against potential discrimination claims.

Structured interviews improve legal defensibility by providing clear documentation that you can reference if someone questions your hiring practices. This transparency protects your organization and ensures fairness. All candidates know the same criteria for judging them.

Now that you understand the importance of structured interviews for fairness and consistency, let's discuss another crucial element in making better hiring decisions: delaying judgment and embracing humility. By taking a step back before forming conclusions, you can improve the quality of your choices and foster more inclusive recruitment practices.

Delaying Judgment and Embracing Humility

This new revolution in service industry hiring challenges the traditional recruiting doctrine. It shifts focus away from the recruiter's "big decision" to hire or not, emphasizing instead the importance of data insights and a carefully structured process.

Delaying judgment and embracing humility in recruitment allows you to develop informed intuition, leading to more informed decisions. By trusting structured data over initial gut feelings, you minimize biases and enhance fairness, creating a more effective and inclusive hiring process.

Withholding Immediate Intuition to Obtain Data and Develop Data Insights

When you rely solely on gut feelings, you risk making snap decisions that may miss essential information about a candidate's capabilities. Imagine you meet an applicant whose personality immediately resonates with you—maybe they remind you of a great former colleague. While it's tempting to trust that instant connection, which is the bias of the halo effect, pausing to review structured data often reveals insights that emotions alone can't provide.

Data-driven hiring helps ensure a complete assessment; going beyond first impressions triggers the halo effect bias to focus on a candidate's measurable qualifications, ultimately leading to better hiring outcomes.

Service industries benefit particularly from this approach. For example, humans' urge to judge is powerful but harmful to recruiting outcomes. If a recruiter consciously rejects "extrapolation" from the few data points and collects all information, then the judgment would be much more accurate, eliminating potential biases.

Faithful Scoring to Predefined Criteria

Scoring candidates against predefined benchmarks is one of the simplest ways to maintain consistency in recruitment. It forces you to evaluate each applicant using the same criteria, leaving less room for bias. Consider a scenario where you need to fill a customer service role and have identified empathy, problem-solving, and communication skills as essential traits. By assigning scores for each skill after interviews, you ensure that every candidate—regardless of their personality or likability—gets evaluated based on what matters most for success in the role.

In the service sector, structured scoring also boosts hiring efficiency, especially in environments with high turnover. Retail and hospitality recruiters, for instance, find that standardizing evaluations helps streamline hiring even under pressure. By using ATSs to support scoring, recruiters can efficiently compare candidates and reduce reliance on memory, which can often be biased or inaccurate.

Reject Initial Gut Feelings and Depend on Informed Intuition

Trusting data more than initial gut feelings doesn't mean abandoning human judgment; instead, it means recognizing where bias and noise could distort your hiring decisions. According to research, as many as 48% of hiring managers admit to unconscious bias during hiring (Richichi, 2023). When you rely on data, you minimize the risk of hiring based on personal preferences, such as choosing candidates with backgrounds or personalities similar to your own.

Service-oriented companies that embrace data over initial gut feelings see measurable benefits. An example from one study showed that using data to improve candidate selection processes resulted in a 20% decrease in employee turnover (Alexander, 2024). Additionally, focusing recruitment efforts on effective channels—determined through data analysis—saves costs and improves hiring speed without sacrificing quality.

Still, intuition plays a vital role in recruiting decisions—just not the initial intuition but the gut feeling. We promote "informed intuition." The intuition developed after reviewing data and understanding its insights. So, the final call is still human judgment but a fully informed one.

While data-driven recruitment enhances objectivity, adding multiple perspectives further strengthens the process. Collaborative decision-making ensures that hiring decisions reflect a balanced consideration of various perspectives, preventing the dominance of one person's biases. Let's explore how teamwork makes recruitment fairer, more strategic, and more balanced.

Collaborative Decision-Making

Collaborative decision-making in recruitment combines diverse perspectives to reduce bias and noise and improve hiring outcomes. By involving multiple evaluators and using methods like anonymous voting, organizations create a fairer, more transparent process that fosters better candidate selection, especially in industries where teamwork and adaptability are essential.

Involving Multiple Evaluators by Soliciting Outside Views

Recruitment decisions become more accurate and fair when multiple evaluators participate. By averaging the evaluation results from multiple evaluators, the noise of recruiting decisions is often minimized. Diverse evaluators average out inherited human noise and bias, leading to a more comprehensive assessment. Structured processes involving multiple evaluators reduce biases, such as affinity or similar-to-me bias, improving fairness and increasing the likelihood of selecting the right candidate.

When you ask someone to make several judgments, they often give varying answers. Averaging these responses increases accuracy because people focus on different factors at different times. Individuals also vary, sometimes in consistent ways. From an organization's perspective, these differences among people create "noise," so averaging helps reduce that noise.

This approach strengthens accountability and transparency. In the service industry, where turnover rates are high, involving multiple raters prevents subjective impressions from dominating decisions. When several evaluators assess candidates, they reduce the risks of cultural bias or favoritism, fostering inclusivity.

Anonymous Voting Processes

Introducing anonymous voting in hiring further reduces bias and noise by allowing evaluators to provide feedback without fear of social or professional pressure. Workplace dynamics can sometimes lead individuals to conform to dominant opinions—particularly those of higher-ranking employees. Anonymity ensures that feedback reflects genuine observations and data-driven judgments, improving the objectivity of the process.

Anonymous evaluations also prevent relational bias, which occurs when personal relationships within the team influence hiring decisions. In the service industry, where teamwork is paramount, maintaining unbiased evaluations ensures that candidates are judged based on skills and potential rather than familiarity or favoritism. This method encourages authentic feedback, fostering fairness and transparency and enhancing trust in the recruitment process.

Structured processes and input from multiple evaluators enhance fairness, but recruitment involves more than analytics. Intuition is vital, especially in assessing soft skills or team dynamics. The real challenge is deciding when to trust your instincts and when to lean on data. Here's how you can balance intuition with structured decision-making effectively.

Appropriate Use of Intuition

When it comes to decision-making, intuition often feels like a natural shortcut. Yet, relying solely on gut instinct can lead to bias and inconsistency, especially in high-stakes decisions. For better outcomes, it's essential to lay a foundation in data before letting intuition play a role. This approach isn't about removing intuition entirely; it's about delaying it until you have a clear, fact-based understanding. Here's how to ensure that intuition complements, rather than overshadows, objective decision-making.

Build a Strong Data Foundation First

Before you let intuition shape your decisions, start with a solid database. Think of data as the groundwork that keeps your intuition anchored. Say you're evaluating job candidates—begin by breaking down the process into objective assessments of each candidate's skills, experience, and attributes. Evaluate each factor individually, aiming to keep your judgments fact-based and distinct.

For example, if one candidate's extensive experience impresses you, resist the urge to let that influence how you view their other qualities, like communication skills or adaptability. Keeping each judgment independent reduces the chance of one positive (or negative) trait skewing your entire perception of the candidate. Independence and fact-based assessments ensure a solid, unbiased starting point.

Delay Intuition, Don't Eliminate It

The goal isn't to eliminate intuition entirely but to delay it until you've processed all relevant information objectively. Picture this as giving yourself time to absorb the data and let it settle before making a gut-level call. Delaying intuition allows for a more thoughtful, disciplined approach, helping you avoid snap judgments that can lead to errors.

Consider the case of a judge in a competition. Instead of making an immediate overall judgment, they could score each performance aspect separately: creativity, skill, presentation, and so on. Independently evaluating these prevents one exceptional or lackluster trait from dominating their entire assessment. When they finally put the scores together to form an intuition about who should win, their judgment will likely be more balanced and reflective of each participant's strengths and weaknesses.

Practice Informed Intuition

Once you've gathered data and taken the time to process it, intuition becomes a helpful tool, providing that "gut check" at this moment that can confirm or raise questions about your initial assessment. When intuition is grounded in informed, data-driven analysis, it often serves as a valuable final lens, helping you see potential red flags or affirm your choice.

For instance, if you're hiring for a critical role and all the data points to a specific candidate, your intuition may still sense a disconnect. This moment of intuitive hesitation isn't something to ignore; instead, treat it as a prompt to review your data once more and double-check for anything you might have overlooked. Intuition can provide that extra layer of confidence if everything still checks out. If not, it may guide you to dig a little deeper.

By incorporating data before intuition, you create a structured decision-making path that balances objectivity and instinct. Rather than being pulled in one direction by instinct, you'll feel grounded by a disciplined approach, allowing intuition to grow from data and data insights rather than a standalone solution.

With a solid data-driven foundation supporting your decisions, it's time to leverage data insights. This next step will show you how to gather and interpret data to enhance every stage of the decision-making process.

Key Takeaways

- Decision hygiene reduces the influence of unconscious biases and noises.

- Structured, collaborative processes lead to better hiring decisions.

- Intuition tends to have less noise and bias only after someone reviews and makes sense of all evaluation data.

With intuition and data working harmoniously, the next step is embracing AI to supercharge recruitment. From streamlining candidate sourcing to eliminating unconscious bias, AI technology offers tools that revolutionize hiring. Let's explore how these innovations are shaping the future of recruitment and empowering HR teams to make smarter, faster decisions.

Chapter 14:

Embracing AI Technology—The

Future of Recruitment

You're sitting in your office, sifting through a mountain of resumes, eyes glazing over. Suddenly, your phone pings—it's a recruiter friend bragging about how AI helped them narrow down the perfect candidates in half the time. You chuckle, thinking about your endless hours playing the "spot the red flag" game on applications. Then it hits you—maybe it's time to let technology lend a hand. Who knew the future could be this efficient?

This chapter highlights how integrating AI technology into your recruitment process boosts efficiency, reduces bias, and supports fairer hiring decisions. You'll learn how AI tools streamline repetitive tasks like resume screening, allowing you to focus on strategic aspects of hiring. AI also enhances decision-making by using data-driven evaluations, helping eliminate hiring bias and promote inclusivity. The chapter explains how AI's standardized assessments improve objectivity and consistency, offering every candidate a fair shot.

By leveraging AI, you create a recruitment process that's faster, more accurate, and more aligned with your company's unique hiring needs.

The Advantages of AI in Recruitment

AI is transforming the recruitment process by enhancing objectivity, increasing efficiency, providing cost-effective solutions, and drastically enhancing the recruiting outcome—better hires, lower training failure rate, lower turnover, and a joyful team. From minimizing biases and speeding up routine tasks to offering data-driven insights, AI empowers recruiters to make more informed and strategic hiring decisions, particularly in service industries where speed and accuracy are vital.

Enhancing Objectivity and Reducing Bias and Noise

One of AI's most compelling advantages to recruitment is its potential to reduce bias and noise and increase objectivity in hiring decisions. Human recruiters can unintentionally let personal biases influence their choices despite their best intentions. These biases, which can stem from a candidate's name, gender, or age, often undermine the fairness of the hiring process, leading to missed opportunities for qualified individuals. This issue is fundamental in the service industry, where having a diverse workforce can improve customer relationships and drive innovation.

AI offers a solution by removing personal bias from the equation. When you use AI to screen resumes, the algorithms focus purely on the qualifications and experience presented, disregarding any personal details that might trigger unconscious bias. Recruiters often overlook highly qualified candidates based on their names, genders, or ethnic backgrounds. By allowing AI to handle this phase, you can foster a more diverse and inclusive workforce based purely on merit.

According to a 2020 McKinsey report, companies with executive teams in the top quartile for gender diversity were 25% more likely to achieve above-average profitability (*Diversity Wins*, 2020). This objectivity is particularly beneficial for recruitment in the service industry, where customer-facing roles benefit from diverse teams.

AI-powered tools like Pymetrics offer a strong example of using neuroscience-based games to evaluate candidates' cognitive and emotional features. The company's human analysts examine the game results without considering personal data, which could lead to biased hiring. This helps recruiters focus on candidates' skills and suitability for the role instead of considering their demographics. It's like having an extra set of eyes that remain objective and focused on finding the best fit, regardless of background.

Be mindful of how developers create AI systems. If a system learns from biased data, it will produce biased outcomes. To avoid this, review the composition of the dataset and test the system's performance across different protected groups, such as race, gender, and ethnicity. Influential AI system builders should use datasets that exclude these protected attributes to prevent bias.

Increasing Efficiency and Speed

Time-consuming tasks are another challenge AI helps resolve. Anyone who's ever screened hundreds of resumes knows how draining and error-prone the process can be. Speed is essential in the fast-paced world of recruitment, especially in industries with high turnover, like hospitality or retail. You must fill roles quickly to avoid service disruptions and ensure smooth operations.

AI streamlines recruitment by handling routine tasks, enabling you to focus on making strategic decisions. Instead of manually reviewing resumes, AI quickly scans thousands of applications and identifies candidates that closely match the job criteria. Tools like HireVue use AI to evaluate video interviews, analyzing tone, word choice, and facial expressions to assess a candidate's fit for the role. This automation minimizes the risk of human error. It ensures you don't miss out on potentially great candidates, all while saving time.

For instance, according to a 2021 Deloitte study, 67% of recruiters believe AI helps improve the efficiency of the hiring process by speeding up tasks like resume sorting and scheduling interviews (Stefanowicz, 2024). Speed is a game-changer in the service industry, where quick hiring can directly impact business operations. A restaurant or hotel can't afford to wait weeks to fill a vacancy, and AI makes it possible to handle large volumes of candidates without sacrificing quality or precision.

Chatbots offer another way AI improves recruitment efficiency. These AI-powered bots communicate with candidates 24/7, answering questions, providing updates, and even handling initial screenings. If you're managing a busy hiring process and a candidate has a question at 2 a.m., the chatbot responds instantly, keeping them engaged and progressing. This continuous interaction helps lower candidate drop-off rates and creates a smoother experience for everyone involved.

This efficiency is crucial in the service industry, where handling large numbers of candidates is common. A retail chain is preparing for the holiday season. AI tools efficiently sort through applications, schedule interviews, and manage candidate communication, freeing recruiters to concentrate on selecting the top talent. By automating these tasks, the process moves faster and prevents hiring team burnout, letting them focus their energy on making final decisions.

Cost-Effectiveness

AI also offers significant cost-saving benefits in recruitment. AI tools require a substantial initial investment, but their long-term savings make them a wise choice. Hiring expenses can quickly escalate in high-turnover industries like hospitality and retail, making efficient solutions essential. AI reduces these costs by streamlining the process and enabling faster, more accurate hiring without relying heavily on manual labor.

AI can also help predict a candidate's tenure longevity, identifying who will likely stay longer and be a better fit for the company culture. According to research from the Talent Board, companies that use AI in recruitment experience 35% faster hiring and a 25% improvement in retention (*New Research Reveals Chatbots*, 2022). This predictive capability can save time and money in a business where constant hiring can drain resources.

Now that you've seen how AI can boost objectivity, efficiency, and cost savings in recruitment, it's time to dive into the specifics of how these technologies work in practice. In the next section, we'll explore AI technologies and how they change the recruitment landscape from top to bottom.

AI Technologies in Action

With AI technologies transforming every industry, recruiting has become one of the fields experiencing substantial changes. AI-driven tools are now at the forefront, enhancing sourcing, evaluating, predicting, and gaining insights into the hiring process. By understanding how each AI function works, you can leverage these tools more effectively and see the impact on the quality of hires, efficiency, and overall recruiting success. Here's how AI enhances each stage of the recruiting process, with a step-by-step breakdown of its application in the hiring pipeline.

Sourcing: Finding the Right Applicants

One of the first areas where AI shines is in sourcing candidates. Sourcing is all about finding suitable applicants based on specific criteria, keywords, and even Boolean search operators to narrow your candidate list. AI tools scan resumes, job boards, and professional networking sites, searching for individuals who match the role requirements. Screening candidates through chatbots or personality assessments further narrows the pool, ensuring you engage with candidates who align with the job and company culture.

Example

Imagine you're hiring for a customer service role. Instead of manually combing through hundreds of resumes, an AI sourcing tool can use specific keywords like "customer experience," "problem-solving," and "empathy" to identify the most promising candidates. A chatbot could then conduct an initial screening, asking questions to gauge each candidate's fit before moving them to the next stage.

Pros

AI sourcing saves recruiters significant time and energy by automating keyword searches and initial screenings. With a targeted approach, you can eliminate guesswork and focus on qualified candidates, speeding up the process.

Cons

However, there's a caveat: A candidate's readiness to find a new job is crucial. If someone's resume matches the job description but is not actively seeking a role, they may never reach the interview stage. Combining job advertisements with resume analysis might help address this limitation, ensuring you reach candidates who are genuinely interested in your role.

Evaluating: Conducting Objective Interviews

AI evaluation tools are changing how interviews are scored and reviewed. AI-powered interview agents, including video and chatbot interview platforms, use natural language processing to assess candidates' responses and assign scores based on predetermined criteria. This brings consistency and accuracy, often tricky for human interviewers to maintain, reducing scoring errors and minimizing bias.

Example

Let's say you're hiring for a leadership position and need someone with excellent communication skills and strategic thinking. An AI interview agent can evaluate the candidate's responses and score factors like clarity, relevance, and depth of answers. It ensures you compare candidates on an even playing field and focus on the competencies that matter most.

Pros

AI improves scoring accuracy, offering a fast, efficient, and unbiased evaluation process. Recruiters get to work with a more objective view of each candidate, which ultimately aids in fairer hiring decisions.

Cons

While chatbot interview agents are impressive, they're still evolving. Humanlike conversations can sometimes feel too scripted or robotic, but the speed of improvement is promising. As AI becomes more conversationally adept, these tools will become even more powerful and engaging for candidates.

Predicting: Making Smarter Hiring Decisions

AI prediction models analyze data from past hires to recommend whether or not a candidate should proceed in the hiring process. Using advanced algorithms, AI can predict a candidate's likelihood of success in a role, improving the quality of hiring decisions and increasing retention rates.

Example

Suppose you're recruiting for a technical position that requires a particular skill set and adaptability. The AI model compares the candidate's profile with previous successful hires and recommends whether they should move forward. This recommendation helps you make better-informed decisions, aligning each hire more closely with the company's needs.

Pros

AI-driven predictions enhance hiring outcomes by helping recruiters make more informed decisions. They analyze vast amounts of data, allowing you to select candidates more likely to succeed based on predictive indicators.

Cons

While AI predictions are robust, a human decision should ultimately validate the AI's recommendation. Combining AI insights with human-informed intuition ensures a balanced approach, as the AI can sometimes miss the subtleties that only human-informed intuition can catch.

Insight: Building Tailored Training and Management Plans

AI doesn't stop at hiring—it also offers valuable insights into each candidate's strengths and areas for improvement, guiding you in structuring onboarding and training programs. By identifying skills gaps and competencies, AI helps managers tailor coaching and development efforts, making for a smoother transition and better long-term performance.

Example

If AI insights identify that an applicant has demonstrated strong analytical skills but may need support in customer service, recruiters and trainers can help design a customized training plan that addresses this specific need. This approach enables new hires to hit the ground running and feel supported in their growth.

Pros

Integrating training and management insights into recruiting helps close the loop, turning recruiting into a continual employee development process. AI provides a "treasure trove" of information that lets you craft more effective training and coaching strategies, enhancing new hire performance.

Cons

Performance tracking is essential for validating AI insights. By following up on new hires' progress, you can assess how well the AI insights match real-world performance, using this data to improve the system further.

With AI making a difference at every stage of recruitment, you're ready to explore how to implement these tools successfully. The next topic covers practical steps for integrating AI solutions into your recruiting process, helping you maximize the technology's potential and see the best results.

Implementing AI Solutions

When implementing AI solutions in recruitment, it's crucial to balance enhancing your processes and addressing potential challenges. By strategically integrating AI and prioritizing data quality, you can significantly improve efficiency while maintaining transparency and fairness in your hiring approach.

Integrating AI Into Existing Processes

When integrating AI into your hiring processes, you need a game plan to make the transition as smooth as possible. Think of your current recruitment structure as a puzzle, where AI is the missing piece that can complete the bigger picture. By identifying the right places to insert AI, you can avoid unnecessary disruptions and ensure efficiency.

Begin by identifying the areas in your recruitment process where AI tools would have the most significant impact. Tasks like resume screening, scheduling interviews, and interacting with candidates via chatbots are ideal for AI integration. For instance, AI-powered systems can quickly analyze thousands of resumes, filtering out unqualified candidates based on specific criteria in a fraction of the time it would take a person. AI can reduce manual screening time in high-volume hiring environments, especially within the service industry. Once you've determined these key areas, gradually implement AI tools to ensure they enhance your current processes without causing disruptions.

The next step is gathering data. Identify the data types you need, set up a structured data collection process, and establish methods to maintain data quality. Review your recruiting pipeline and implement a solid data infrastructure.

Effective data collection and management are critical in making AI function properly. AI relies on quality data to deliver meaningful results. Even the most advanced AI systems without accurate information can't provide valuable outcomes. Regular audits of your data sources are vital to maintaining consistency and reliability. Companies using consistent and trustworthy data saw an increase in AI-driven hiring success. Keeping data entry uniform throughout recruitment helps AI learn from structured, reliable information.

Addressing Challenges and Considerations

Although AI offers many advantages, you need to stay aware of potential challenges and ethical concerns. AI has flaws; adopting it without careful planning can create privacy, security, and bias issues.

Bias in AI systems is a noteworthy point. Since AI relies on historical data, it often repeats and even amplifies existing biases. For instance, a major tech company had to stop using its AI recruitment tool because it favored male candidates over female ones. This highlights the need for regular testing and auditing of AI systems to maintain fairness. Organizations should create clear guidelines for AI use and ensure they are transparent to both teams and candidates. According to HireVue, openly discussing AI's role in hiring helps build trust and enhances the candidate experience (LeFebvre, 2024).

You should implement policies to safeguard candidate data. Addressing privacy concerns, particularly when handling sensitive personal information, is essential. Ensure that the data you collect is always encrypted and that your AI systems follow local and international regulations, such as the General Data Protection Regulation.

Training your team to use AI technology effectively is essential. Introducing advanced tools is just the first step; ensuring everyone knows how to use them is just as important. Begin by assessing your team's skills, then provide targeted training through interactive workshops or webinars. Using real-life examples, like how AI automates tasks such as scheduling interviews, helps recruiters focus on strategic work, like building candidate relationships. Recruiters using AI have more time to engage with candidates, enhancing the overall hiring experience.

Employees may resist AI, fearing that automation will take over their jobs. Reassure them by emphasizing that AI assists rather than replaces. It manages routine tasks, freeing your team to concentrate on higher-value work.

Finally, appoint change champions within your organization—individuals who understand recruitment and AI technologies and can serve as advocates for the integration process. These champions can help guide other team members, offering practical insights and dispelling myths about AI. For example, suppose a recruiter is skeptical about chatbots' effectiveness in candidate engagement. In that case, a change champion can demonstrate how chatbots can streamline communication, ensuring no candidate gets left behind.

Feedback loops are essential as you adopt AI. Regularly check in with your recruitment team to assess AI's impact on workflow and candidate experience. Is the AI delivering the results you expected? Are there areas for improvement? By maintaining open channels for feedback, you ensure that your AI tools stay relevant and practical, adapting as your recruitment needs evolve.

Building your AI infrastructure can require a significant initial investment.

A more innovative option is to use turnkey solutions from platforms like EmployJoy.ai. This software-as-a-service platform provides a tailored recruiting pipeline, proven interview questions with scoring systems, and AI prediction models specifically designed for the service industry.

This approach avoids heavy upfront costs. Instead, a monthly subscription lets you transform your hiring process and achieve powerful results.

Now that you've laid the groundwork for integrating AI into your hiring processes and considered the challenges, it's time to look at the bigger picture. How exactly does AI impact recruitment outcomes? Let's dive into how these technological tools can transform your results, making your recruitment efforts more precise and productive.

The Impact on Recruitment Outcomes

AI is transforming recruitment by improving accuracy in candidate selection and significantly reducing the time-to-hire. These advancements are particularly impactful in industries like hospitality and retail, where high turnover and urgent hiring demands require innovative solutions that boost efficiency and quality in the hiring process.

Improved Accuracy in Candidate Selection

Traditional recruitment often depends on a recruiter's intuition and experience. Still, even the best recruiters can overlook important patterns in resumes. AI improves candidate selection accuracy by quickly analyzing data and reviewing resumes, job descriptions, and social media profiles to find candidates whose skills and experiences best fit the role.

For example, in the service industry—where turnover is high, and skills need to match specific customer service standards—AI can quickly sift through giant pools of applicants. It looks for patterns in qualifications, past job performance, and even personality traits, matching suitable candidates to the roles that best fit their strengths. This makes better hires more likely to excel and stay longer, reducing the constant churn many service-based companies face.

Organizations using AI in recruitment saw an improvement in hiring quality. AI systems can dig deeper into data than a recruiter might during an initial resume scan. For instance, while you might overlook a candidate because of an unconventional job history, an AI algorithm could recognize a transferable skill or a relevant experience you wouldn't have considered.

AI improves skill matching and helps reduce unconscious biases in hiring. AI focuses on objective, data-driven criteria, helping to reduce the influence of factors like gender, race, or background that may unintentionally affect human decisions. Companies can monitor and adjust AI systems to maintain fairness, as these tools can sometimes inherit biases from training data. When managed effectively, AI is a powerful tool for creating more diverse and inclusive workplaces.

Focusing on diversity can lead to significant gains in representation in the service industry. A McKinsey report reveals that companies in the top quartile for racial and ethnic diversity are 35% more likely to achieve higher financial returns (Hunt et al., 2015). Your team improves hiring accuracy by leveraging AI to make objective hiring decisions. It builds a workforce that better represents your customer base.

Reduce Recruiting, Training, and Turnover Costs, and Increase Profitability

The financial impact of faster, better hiring decisions is substantial in the service industry. Consider the costs that quickly add up:

Total Cost per Turnover

Category	Amount	Note
Recruiting Cost	$4,700	SHRM, Society for Human Resource Management.
Revenue Loss - Opportunity Cost	$6,000	Assuming recruiting and training time of 1 month and a daily revenue impact of $300.
Training Cost	$1,096	https://trainingmag.com/: average traing cost for a small company.
Cost of the Time to Full Productivity	$6,240	Assuming it takes the average new employee two month to fully onboard and fully productive. Assuming a fully loaded hourly pay rate of $19.5 per hour.
Total Cost of Turnover	$18,036	

- **Direct recruiting cost:** Advertising, interview hours, and onboarding expenses contribute to a significant hiring price tag.

- **Revenue loss (opportunity cost):** Every unfilled position affects productivity, reducing potential revenue.

- **Training cost:** New hires need onboarding and role-specific training, a direct hit to your training budget.

- **Cost of time to full productivity:** Getting new employees up to speed takes time, delaying optimal performance and profitability.

Reducing monthly turnover from 15% to 12% in a 30-person service company can generate significant savings, totaling approximately $194,000 annually (Bonifacio, 2024). These savings, combined with streamlined processes, significantly boost profitability.

While investing in advanced hiring systems, such as AI, might seem costly upfront, it's often more feasible than expected. Platforms like EmployJoy.ai offer affordable, ready-to-deploy solutions tailored to the service industry, with custom recruiting pipelines, proven interview scoring, and predictive AI models. Rather than high upfront costs, a monthly subscription lets you enhance hiring processes and see impressive returns.

You're already on the path to profitability by reducing recruiting and turnover costs. Next, let's examine how cutting down the time-to-hire can drive even greater efficiency and financial gain.

Reduced Time-To-Hire

Sorting through hundreds or thousands of applications can make recruiting time-consuming. HR teams in fast-paced industries like hospitality and retail often deal with high turnover and the ongoing pressure to fill roles quickly. AI speeds up the hiring process while ensuring quality remains intact.

AI tools automate repetitive tasks that often slow down the recruitment process. For example, AI filters candidates based on specific criteria instead of requiring recruiters to review resumes manually. This enables recruiters to reduce time spent on initial screenings and dedicate more effort to connecting with the top candidates.

Take resume screening. This can take hours in a typical recruitment cycle, with HR professionals weeding out unqualified candidates individually. But AI can handle that same task in minutes, combing through a mountain of applications and pulling out the most relevant ones based on skills, experience, and even soft skills that align with the job description.

In the service industry, where time is crucial, this speed becomes invaluable as employers need to fill positions quickly. A 2021 LinkedIn study found that AI recruitment tools can cut time-to-hire by up to 50% (Behr, n.d.). Filling roles faster improves the candidate experience, which is crucial to attracting top talent. Candidates don't want to wait weeks for feedback, and AI helps keep them engaged and interested by speeding up the process.

Hilton Hotels used AI-driven recruitment tools to significantly reduce the time it took to fill its service positions. Its HR team reported that AI reduced the average hiring time by 40% (D'Cruz, 2023). This was possible by automating tasks like resume screening, interview scheduling, and chat-based assessments.

AI speeds up the hiring process and reduces the burden on your HR team. By automating routine tasks, your team can concentrate on building relationships with candidates and enhancing recruitment strategies. This shift enhances operational efficiency and leads to improved hiring results, as companies using AI in recruitment often see increased team productivity.

AI provides a crucial advantage for the service industry, where high turnover costs and positions often need filling immediately. By cutting the time-to-hire in half, you can stay ahead of the competition, ensuring that your business continues to run smoothly without the headaches of being short-staffed.

Key Takeaways

- AI enhances recruitment by providing data-driven, unbiased insights.

- Proper implementation of AI tools leads to better hiring decisions.

- Awareness of AI limitations ensures responsible and effective use.

- AI implementation can drastically reduce costs and increase profitability.

Now that you've seen how AI can boost accuracy and speed in hiring, it's time to address the bigger picture. Many recruitment challenges stem from chaotic processes and false promises. The next chapter will break down common pains, debunk misleading solutions, and outline a clear path forward.

Chapter 15:

From Chaos to Clarity—

Summarizing Pains, False

Solutions, and the Path Forward

You sit at your desk, surrounded by a mountain of resumes, each promising to be the "perfect fit." After days of interviews, you finally hire someone who seemed like a good match—only for them to quit two weeks later, claiming they found their "true calling" in a different industry. You start feeling like recruitment is an endless loop of chaos and setbacks. But there's a better way forward—it's not about quick fixes but strategic solutions that bring lasting clarity.

Let's examine your recruitment challenges more closely and identify ways to turn them into strategic opportunities for success.

Revisiting the Recruitment Challenges

The recruiting system in the service industry is overdue for a complete overhaul. Many recruitment practices today can't meet the demands of fast-paced service environments. From high turnover to slow hiring, these issues point to a need for revolutionary changes in how talent is sourced, trained, and retained.

Failing to Deliver Great Hires

The current recruitment process often results in too many training failures and high turnover, even among employees who initially seem like a good fit. Imagine hiring someone, investing in their training, and then seeing them leave within a few months. Not only is this frustrating, but it also creates ongoing staffing gaps that disrupt operations and impact customer service quality. Consistent turnover and mismatches drain resources and morale in a sector where reliability and customer satisfaction are everything. A more effective recruitment system would focus on identifying and attracting people with the right skills and mindset to succeed in these roles long-term.

Slow Hiring Doesn't Meet Business Needs

Today's recruitment processes are also notoriously slow, creating a time lag that makes it challenging to keep up with staffing needs. Glassdoor reports that hiring in the US typically takes 23 days (*Interview Process*, 2015). Lowering hiring standards to bring more people on board may seem like a quick fix, but it ultimately creates more problems than it solves. Businesses often have higher turnover and less productivity when they settle for candidates without complete qualifications. Instead of lowering standards, the service industry needs faster, more innovative hiring practices, prioritizing finding the right people promptly.

The Toll on Recruiters: Burnout and Unsustainable Workloads

Service industry recruiters face a challenging work environment marked by long hours, high pressure, and constant demands to fill roles. The relentless cycle of sourcing, screening, hiring, and replacing employees leads to burnout and high self-doubt. Recruiters often question their effectiveness and feel like they're one step behind. This pressure and frequent feelings of failure when hires don't work out make the role exhausting and unsustainable. When recruiters experience burnout, the overall effectiveness of the recruitment process declines, resulting in increased turnover and dissatisfaction for both candidates and employers.

High Costs of Recruitment, Training, and Turnover

With so many issues in the hiring process, it's no surprise that the costs associated with recruiting, training, and turnover are incredibly high. Every time a new employee joins and undergoes training, the business takes on considerable costs. When that employee leaves after a short time, those costs effectively double, as the cycle begins again with a new hire. Not only are financial resources drained, but so are valuable time and morale. These costs highlight the urgent need for a new approach emphasizing retention and sustainability rather than constantly starting from scratch.

Given these challenges, recruitment practices in the service industry need more than minor adjustments—they need a complete transformation. Only a revolutionary approach, grounded in new methods, data-driven strategies, and sustainable practices, can address the root issues and create a recruiting system that benefits everyone involved.

Given the clear need for change, let's examine previous ineffective solutions. Reflecting on these approaches can help guide us toward strategies that will genuinely address the challenges in service industry recruiting.

Reflecting on Ineffective Solutions

It's easy to seek quick fixes when faced with recruiting challenges. However, these fixes often not only address the core issues but can also change problems. Let's look at some common yet misguided solutions and why taking a fresh approach is essential to making meaningful progress.

Just Working Harder Isn't Enough

Putting in more hours or pushing yourself harder can feel like the correct answer when things aren't going well. But with a new framework or strategy, this effort can yield the results you're hoping for. Picture yourself trying to empty a sinking ship with nothing more than a small bucket. Working faster will temporarily help, but you will waste the effort without addressing the hole in the boat. To solve core issues in recruiting, you need a different approach altogether—working harder alone won't fill the gaps that a new, strategic perspective could close.

Lowering Hiring Standards Is a Costly Quick Fix

When the pressure to fill roles quickly mounts, lowering hiring standards is a tempting shortcut. This approach can result in expensive turnover and missed opportunities. When a less-than-ideal hire doesn't work out, you face rehiring expenses, potential dips in team morale, and possible impacts on your company's reputation. Research consistently shows that high turnover can erode morale and affect overall productivity (Lepak, 2024). So, rather than compromising standards to make quick hires, focus on building a robust and sustainable recruitment process that attracts suitable candidates.

Rethinking the Reliance on Gut Feelings

Recruiters often lean heavily on intuition when evaluating candidates. While instinct and experience can undoubtedly play a role, relying solely on "gut feelings" is a practice that falls short in today's data-driven world. If Henry Ford had only focused on making faster horses, he would have missed the opportunity to create the automobile. Similarly, the recruitment field thrives when we shift away from solely relying on personal judgment and embrace modern tools and data-driven insights. This shift can help remove bias and increase accuracy, creating a better match between candidates and roles. For example, data-backed assessment tools can help reveal candidate potential that intuition alone might overlook (*Leveraging Data-Driven Insights*, 2024).

Faster Horses vs Vehicles

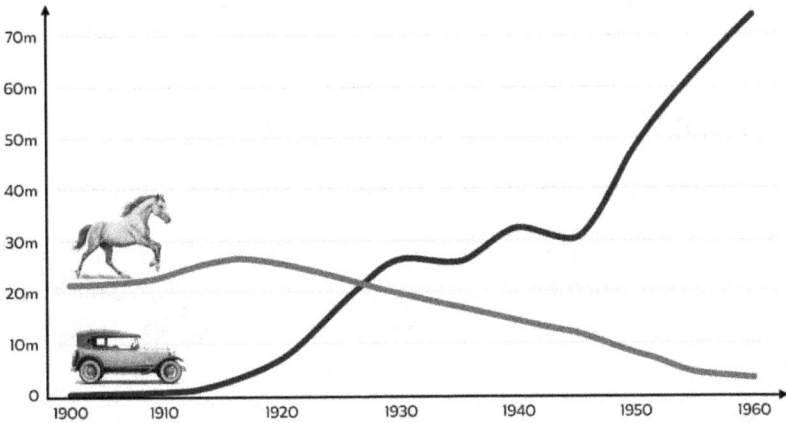

Source: Kilby,E.R. (2007). The demographics of the U.S. equine population.

The Struggle Without Data Insights

Operating without solid data insights is like navigating through thick fog. Decisions often rely on guesswork, leading to inconsistencies and preventing you from fully optimizing your recruitment strategy. Embracing data insights enables you to understand patterns in your hiring process, measure the success of different approaches, and identify areas for improvement. Organizations using data-driven hiring techniques have a clearer picture of what works, allowing them to make smarter, more informed decisions. Without data, you're navigating in the dark, unable to assess your efforts' impact accurately.

To overcome these challenges, embracing a revolutionary approach to recruiting is essential. Moving beyond traditional, labor-intensive methods and making data-driven decisions saves time, reduces turnover, and leads to a more efficient and impactful hiring process. By adopting this new paradigm, you equip your team with tools that drive better results, ensure quality hires, and strengthen your organization's reputation.

Having highlighted ineffective solutions, let's now shift to what truly works. Emphasizing strategies that leverage data, focus on quality, and drive impactful outcomes will take your recruiting process to the next level. Let's explore how these practical strategies can transform your approach and lead to lasting success.

Emphasizing Effective Strategies

You need a well-rounded strategy to build a recruitment process that attracts the right talent and supports long-term retention. This strategy incorporates proven practical behavioral science, behavioral economics, data science, and AI solutions. It involves designing clear job roles, evaluating candidates thoughtfully, leveraging data and technology, and maintaining objective decision-making practices to build a strong, committed, and joyful workforce.

Effective Job Design Based on Targeted Application Segments

A solid job description is essential for attracting high-quality candidates. It's like a perfectly tailored suit—it fits the role precisely. It draws in the candidates best suited for the position. To design job descriptions that resonate with your target segments, focus on the specific skills, experiences, and qualities needed for each role. For example, if hiring customer service reps for a hospitality business, emphasize traits like empathy, communication, and problem-solving. This tailored approach not only filters out unsuitable candidates but also sets the tone for the type of culture they can expect.

Turnover rates tend to be high in the service industry. Hence, it is crucial to design job descriptions highlighting the role and advantages based on applicant segments and company core values. Job postings with clearly defined competitive advantages receive more applications. Transparency and engagement can attract candidates who genuinely resonate with your company's mission and values.

Skin-In-The-Game Recruiting Process

As discussed, skin-in-the-game recruiting streamlines the process by using intelligent, straightforward checkpoints that allow applicants to self-select if they're not genuinely committed, saving you time and energy by filtering out unqualified candidates early on. You can start with brief, purposeful tasks, like a quick survey or a few SMS questions, to gauge commitment immediately. Only those who genuinely want the job will try to respond, giving you an early indicator of professionalism and engagement. By setting these small self-selection tasks at every stage of the process, you automatically filter out uncommitted applicants, focusing your time on candidates who have shown they're serious and ready for the role.

Work smarter, not harder, and let the process naturally highlight the best fits!

The Fine Balance of Screening and Advocating

Finding the right candidate for service roles means more than just screening for skills; it's about understanding what makes the role a win for both the company and the applicant. Balancing objective assessment with advocacy allows you to match candidates' technical and interpersonal strengths while promoting the job's unique benefits in a way that resonates with their needs. By tailoring job details—like consistent hours for working parents or growth opportunities for career-driven applicants—you attract quality candidates who'll thrive in the role.

Advocating the job's strengths requires subtlety; overpromotion can feel like a hard sell, which may put off candidates. Instead, create a smooth, two-way interaction, emphasizing the role's benefits based on each candidate's journey. This balanced, systematic approach fosters trust and leads to more substantial, long-term recruitment success.

Leveraging Data Insights

Data is your best friend when it comes to making informed recruitment decisions. You can use technology and analytics to refine and improve your hiring strategy, ensuring more data-driven and effective choices. Recruitment data can help you track the success of your job postings, the effectiveness of different sourcing channels, and the overall candidate experience.

For example, analytics might show that applicants from one job board have a higher success rate than others, allowing you to focus your efforts on the platforms that work.

Data helps you uncover biases that can emerge in the hiring process. By analyzing patterns and trends, you can spot areas where biases may influence decisions, allowing you to take corrective actions to create a fairer recruitment system. For instance, tracking diversity metrics across candidate pools ensures your outreach is broad enough, helping you build a more inclusive workforce. You can adapt your hiring strategy by continuously analyzing data to better meet your organization's needs.

Ensuring Decision Hygiene

In recruitment, decision-making can be prone to biases and hasty judgments, especially in industries where hiring needs are urgent. Decision hygiene keeps decision-making processes clean and objective, avoiding biases, noises, and external influences.

One way to promote decision hygiene is to use structured interview templates for all candidates. This ensures that every applicant is evaluated against the same criteria, reducing the chances of subjective preferences influencing the outcome. Structured interviews can also increase hiring accuracy compared to unstructured ones.

To keep recruitment decisions objective, consider adding an outside view by involving a hiring committee. A group approach can counter individual biases, offering varied perspectives to create a more balanced evaluation. Another effective practice is anonymous voting processes, where team members rate candidates without knowing others' opinions. This reduces bias and ensures that decisions stem from each member's honest assessment, not group dynamics or external influences. Together, these steps support decision hygiene, keeping your hiring process clean, fair, and focused on finding the best fit for the role.

Deploying AI Technology

AI has become a game-changer in recruitment, especially for service industries with high-volume hiring needs. AI handles repetitive tasks such as screening resumes, scheduling interviews, and conducting preliminary assessments, streamlining these steps in the hiring process. AI in recruitment streamlines sourcing, evaluating, predicting, and onboarding by automating keyword searches, scoring interviews, predicting success, and providing insights for tailored training. This data-driven approach enhances hiring speed, accuracy, and candidate alignment while balancing AI's capabilities with human judgment for a well-rounded, effective recruiting process.

But beyond efficiency, AI also helps with accuracy. For example, AI algorithms can evaluate candidates based on various factors, including past performance data and personality traits, to match them to the best roles. This allows companies to make faster, well-informed hiring choices.

Human intuition and AI can work together to make better decisions. By starting with AI's data-driven insights, you create a grounded foundation, letting intuition complement rather than control choices. This balance allows intuition to serve as a thoughtful "gut check," refining AI's objective analysis without letting bias lead.

One Path Forward: Transform Your Hiring Process With AI

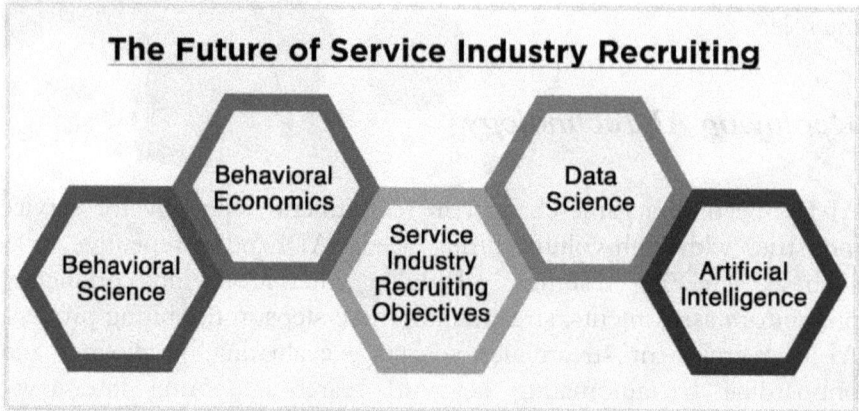

The Future of Service Industry Recruiting

Behavioral Economics

Data Science

Behavioral Science

Service Industry Recruiting Objectives

Artificial Intelligence

Revolutionizing recruitment with data-driven strategies and AI technology is the key to making better hiring decisions, reducing turnover, and building a workplace where employees genuinely thrive. You can take one of two routes to make this change: build an in-house system or use a ready-made solution. Either path empowers you to hire faster and more effectively, creating a happy, efficient team.

Build an In-House System for Complete Control

Creating a custom recruiting system within your company strengthens core competencies and allows for complete control over data and processes. Here's what you need to make it work:

- **A knowledgeable leader:** You don't need a profoundly technical expert; instead, look for a leader who understands recruiting, data, and AI within a strategic business context. Study programs like MIT's Artificial Intelligence: Implications for Business Strategy provide an excellent training course. A leader with a firm grasp of AI's impact on business can guide this transformation.

- **An investment in the future:** While AI costs have decreased, building your AI recruiting capability requires a substantial investment, potentially over $50,000 (Sheykin, 2024). With this commitment, you elevate your company from simply making hiring improvements to creating a revolutionary, enduring advantage—think of it as upgrading from a "faster horse" to an "automobile."

- **A shift in recruiter mindset:** AI-driven recruiting requires recruiters to go beyond intuition, blending personal insight with data-driven decision-making. This mindset shift—from "I" to "data insights and I"—means recruiters can find the most suitable candidates faster and more accurately.

- **Data science and AI specialists:** These experts bring essential technical skills, guiding data structure, data quality, and modeling. Equipped with at least a bachelor's degree and relevant experience, they ensure your AI system operates efficiently and seamlessly.

- **Using proven AI tools:** Many AI tools are available to streamline and enhance recruiting, from resume screening to interview chatbots. Leveraging these can reduce initial costs and help you build a strong foundation.

Investing in an in-house AI recruiting system gives you a potent competitive edge, positioning your company at the forefront of hiring innovation.

Fast-Track With Turnkey AI Solutions

If building an in-house system feels overwhelming, consider turnkey solutions offered by AI startups. EmployJoy.ai provides tailored recruiting pipelines, automated scoring systems, and AI-driven prediction models specifically for industries like the service sector. Here's why this path might suit you better:

- **No heavy upfront costs:** With a turnkey solution like EmployJoy.ai, founded by the author of this guide, you pay a monthly fee instead of committing to a hefty initial investment. These solutions often include onboarding to set up data infrastructure, recruiting pipelines, interview questions pretested by AI, and extensive recruiting data.

- **Rapid implementation:** Using an established service means quickly improving your recruiting process without waiting for in-house development. This approach is faster, cheaper, and gives you instant access to AI-powered recruiting benefits.

- **Mindset still matters:** Even with a turnkey system, recruiters need to embrace data insights alongside their intuition. This blend ensures you make the most of AI tools, honing a faster and more effective selection process.

Advancements in behavioral science, data science, and AI have reshaped how we work, live, and—now—how we hire. It's time to embrace this transformation. Choosing the right AI strategy for your company will speed up hiring, make smarter choices, and build a team ready to thrive.

Key Takeaways

- Addressing root causes is essential for resolving recruitment challenges.

- Revolutionize service industry recruiting with a data-driven process, leading to exceptional hiring success.

- Innovating and continuously improving helps your business stay competitive over the long term.

- There are two basic approaches to embracing this revolution.

- Recruiting is a game of probabilities. You want to play to win. But, you want to play it in a more favorable position—which is what this book is about.

By implementing comprehensive strategies and embracing continuous improvement, you transform your recruitment process into a powerful tool for long-term success. You're not just filling vacancies—building a resilient team supporting your business goals. This balanced approach ensures we meet immediate and future needs efficiently and purposefully.

Author Bio

Wells Ye: A Visionary Leader in the Service Industry

Wells Ye brings over 20 years of recruiting, management, and service industry innovation expertise. Throughout his career, he has demonstrated strategic leadership, successfully managing a $500 million service contract portfolio for a Fortune 500 company. His ability to lead operations in the trenches underscores his talent for building sustainable and efficient business solutions.

As an entrepreneur, Wells founded multiple service companies, each a testament to his investment in solving one of the industry's toughest challenges—recruitment. He has personally hired more than 2,000 managers, associates, and front-line employees, ensuring his businesses meet their talent needs and operational goals. His hands-on approach and personal commitment to his businesses inspire others to invest their passion and dedication in their work.

Wells' academic background is a testament to his unwavering commitment to innovation built on data science, AI, and trench work in the front line. He earned an MBA from the Wharton School of the University of Pennsylvania, showcasing his strong business acumen. To further enhance his knowledge in technology, he pursued executive education in data strategy at the University of California (Berkeley), artificial intelligence for leaders at the University of Texas at Austin, and marketing AI at Cornell University. These credentials demonstrate his dedication and ability to adapt and innovate, ensuring he can transform recruitment practices in a rapidly changing industry.

Leveraging his expertise in data science and AI, Wells developed the world's first hire-or-not-hire AI decision model. This groundbreaking innovation has revolutionized service sector hiring. This innovative model cut time-to-hire by 66% and reduced employee turnover by 50%, setting new standards for efficiency and success in recruitment. Motivated by these achievements, he launched EmployJoy.ai, a company focused on helping service businesses hire more innovatively and faster, thereby reshaping the industry's approach to recruitment.

Wells lives with his wife and son in Evanston, IL, where he balances his professional success with a meaningful family life. His journey, which is deeply rooted in his family values, exemplifies how leadership, innovation, and dedication can transform industries and positively impact the lives of countless employees and businesses.

References

About stress at work. (2024, February 13). CDC. https://www.cdc.gov/niosh/stress/about/index.html

Alexander, J. (2024, May 22). *How job data analytics for recruitment strategies are revolutionizing.* Jobspikr.com. https://www.jobspikr.com/blog/job-data-analytics-for-recruitment-strategies/

Allen, D. G. (n.d.). *Retaining talent: A guide to analyzing and managing employee turnover.* Society of Human Resource Management. https://www.shrm.org/content/dam/en/shrm/topics-tools/news/Retaining-Talent.pdf

Ankum, M. (2023, March 4). *People analytics: 5 real case studies.* Effectory. https://www.effectory.com/knowledge/people-analytics-5-real-case-studies/

Armstrong, P. (2023, November 21). *How this organisation used AI to cut down time to hire by 20 per cent.* HRM. https://www.hrmonline.com.au/technology/ai-cuts-talent-acquisition-time/

Ayade, P. (2024, June 12). *The rise of AI-powered talent management: Enhancing candidate experiences.* HR Tech Series. https://techrseries.com/featured/the-rise-of-ai-powered-talent-management-enhancing-candidate-experiences/

Batista, E. (2021, February 5). *Daniel Kahneman on conducting better interviews.* Ed Batista. https://www.edbatista.com/2021/02/daniel-kahneman-on-conducting-better-interviews.html

Behr, S. (n.d.). *Reduce time to hire by 50%*. Fountain. https://www.fountain.com/posts/how-to-reduce-time-to-hire-rates-by-50

Beware of candidates who say "always" and "never" in interviews. (n.d.). *Leadership IQ*. https://www.leadershipiq.com/blogs/leadershipiq/beware-candidates-who-say-always-and-never-in-interviews

Bonifacio, R. (2024, October 23). *Reducing employee turnover: Strategies & impact on business*. Shiftbase. https://www.shiftbase.com/glossary/employee-turnover

Burn-out an "occupational phenomenon": International classification of diseases. (2019, May 28). World Health Organization. https://www.who.int/news/item/28-05-2019-burn-out-an-occupational-phenomenon-international-classification-of-diseases

Candidate experience metrics: Elevating recruitment & abandonment rate insights. (n.d.). *Sapia.ai*. https://sapia.ai/resources/blog/recruitment-metrics-how-and-why-to-track-your-candidate-abandonment-rate/

Carillo-Tudela, C., Gartner, H., & Kaas, L. (2020, May). *Recruitment policies, job-filling rates and matching efficiency*. Institute of Labor Economics. https://www.iza.org/publications/dp/13240/recruitment-policies-job-filling-rates-and-matching-efficiency

Carnahan, B., & Moore, C. (2023, June 16). *Actively addressing unconscious bias in recruiting*. Harvard Business School. https://www.hbs.edu/recruiting/insights-and-advice/blog/post/actively-addressing-unconscious-bias-in-recruiting

Caucci, S. (2021, March 15). 10 facts you should know about employee turnover. *1Huddle.* https://1huddle.co/blog/10-facts-you-should-know-about-employee-turnover/

Chen, Z. (2023). Collaboration among recruiters and artificial intelligence: removing human prejudices in employment. *Cognition, Technology, & Work, 25,* 135-149. https://doi.org/10.1007/s10111-022-00716-0

Clayton, J. (2017, May 15). *The five: Reasons your candidates are rejecting your offer.* Recruiting Daily. https://recruitingdaily.com/why-candidates-are-rejecting-your-offer/

Cynkar, A. (2007, April 1). *A towering figure.* American Psychological Association. https://www.apa.org/monitor/apr07/towering

D'Cruz, J. (2023, March 22). *The impact of artificial intelligence on recruiting.* RecruitingDaily. https://recruitingdaily.com/the-impact-of-artificial-intelligence-on-recruiting/

De Smet, A., Dowling, B., Mugayar-Baldocchi, M., & Spratt, J. (2022, January 13). *It's not about the office, it's about belonging.* McKinsey & Company. https://www.mckinsey.com/capabilities/people-and-organizational-performance/our-insights/the-organization-blog/its-not-about-the-office-its-about-belonging

Diversity wins: How inclusion matters. (2020, December 16). Unstereotype Alliance. https://www.unstereotypealliance.org/en/resources/diversity-and-inclusion/2020/12/diversity-wins-report-by-mckinsey

Dong, R., Wu, H., Ni, S., & Lu, T. (2023). The nonlinear consequences of working hours for job satisfaction: The moderating role of job autonomy. *Current Psychology, 42,* 11849-11870. https://doi.org/10.1007/s12144-021-02463-3

Employee Turnover - The hidden costs of attrition. (2021, December 17). Think 3D Solutions. https://letsthink3d.com/blog/the-hidden-costs-of-attrition/

Eser, A. (2024a, July 23). *Industry employee turnover rates revealed: Statistics across various sectors.* World Metrics. https://worldmetrics.org/employee-turnover-by-industry-statistics/

Eser, A. (2024b, July 25). *Employer branding statistics statistics.* ZipDo. https://zipdo.co/employer-branding-statistics/

Farris, S. P. (2022, May 12). 25 hiring statistics all employers should know in 2022. *CareerPlug.* https://www.careerplug.com/blog/hiring-statistics/

Farris, S. P. (2024, March 25). Recruiting metrics benchmarks - Applicant to hire ratio, time to hire & other KPIs. *CareerPlug.* https://www.careerplug.com/blog/recruiting-metrics-and-kpis/

Fennell, A. (2022, March). *Candidate experience statistics 2024.* StandOut CV. https://standout-cv.com/candidate-experience-statistics

Ferguson, S., & Hoover, M. (2024, August 28). *Understanding America's labor shortage: The most impacted industries.* U.S. Chamber of Commerce. https://www.uschamber.com/workforce/understanding-americas-labor-shortage-the-most-impacted-industries

Forgetting curve. (n.d.). Training Industry. https://trainingindustry.com/wiki/content-development/forgetting-curve/

Freifeld, L. (2016, November 10). 2016 training industry report. *Training Mag.* https://trainingmag.com/2o16-training-industry-report/

Fry, R. (2018, April 11). *Millennials are the largest generation in the U.S. labor force.* Pew Research Center. https://www.pewresearch.org/short-reads/2018/04/11/millennials-largest-generation-us-labor-force/

Fuentes, L. (2023, November 16). *Hilton named no. 1 best place to work in the world.* Stories From Hilton. https://stories.hilton.com/releases/hilton-named-no-1-best-place-to-work-in-the-world

Gansser, K. (2023, April 18). *Why restaurants are struggling to find and keep employees.* Fourth. https://www.fourth.com/article/reasons-restaurants-short-staffed

Half, R. (2016, September 23). *How a long recruitment process can hurt you.* Robert Half. https://www.roberthalf.com/us/en/insights/management-tips/how-a-long-recruitment-process-can-hurt-you

Half, R. (2019, May 15). *Cold feet: Survey shows 28% of professionals renege on job offer after accepting.* Newsroom. https://press.roberthalf.com/2019-05-15-Cold-Feet-Survey-Shows-28-Of-Professionals-Renege-On-Job-Offer-After-Accepting

Hernandez, J. (2024, April 11). *White-sounding names get called back for jobs more than Black ones, a new study finds.* Oregon Public Broadcasting. https://www.opb.org/article/2024/04/11/white-sounding-names-get-called-back-for-jobs-more-than-black-ones-a-new-study-finds/

How long should your interview process take? We found out. (2017, August 9). *Glassdoor.* https://www.glassdoor.com/blog/how-long-should-interviews-take/

How stress affects your health. (2022, October 31). American Psychological Association. https://www.apa.org/topics/stress/health

Hunt, D. V., Layton, D., & Prince, S. (2015, January 1). *Why diversity matters.* McKinsey & Company. https://www.mckinsey.com/capabilities/people-and-organizational-performance/our-insights/why-diversity-matters

Hunt, D. V., Yee, L., Prince, S., & Dixon-Fyle, S. (2018, January 18). *Delivering growth through diversity in the workplace.* McKinsey & Company. https://www.mckinsey.com/capabilities/people-and-organizational-performance/our-insights/delivering-through-diversity

Hyatt announces Hyatt Thrive, comprehensive corporate responsibility framework that helps improve local communities, environment worldwide. (2011, June 10). Hyatt Newsroom. https://newsroom.hyatt.com/2011-06-10-HYATT-ANNOUNCES-HYATT-THRIVE-COMPREHENSIVE-CORPORATE-RESPONSIBILITY-FRAMEWORK-THAT-HELPS-IMPROVE-LOCAL-COMMUNITIES-ENVIRONMENT-WORLDWIDE

The importance of employee retention in the hospitality industry: Strategies for HR professionals. (2023, May 25). *HR Cloud.* https://www.hrcloud.com/blog/the-importance-of-employee-retention-in-the-hospitality-industry-strategies-for-hr-professionals

Interview process now averages 22 days: Report. (2015, June 18). Canadian HR Reporter. https://www.hrreporter.com/news/hr-news/interview-process-now-averages-22-days-report/281042

Interview statistics (2024 Updated). (2023, June 23). *Zirtual.* https://www.zirtual.com/blog/interview-statistics/

Jendriks, T. (2023, October 27). 200 recruitment statistics: Trends, problems, and strategies. *Flair.hr*. https://flair.hr/en/blog/recruitment-statistics/

Job interview statistics: Applications and hiring rates in 2024. (n.d.). TeamStage. https://teamstage.io/job-interview-statistics/

Jones, A. (n.d.). *The restaurant labor shortage: How we got here and a 2023 update*. OpenTable for Restaurants. https://restaurant.opentable.com/resources/restaurant-labor-shortage/

Keller, D. (2022, September 1). The mythical man month: 5 lessons about software development. *Five*. https://five.co/blog/5-lessons-on-software-development-the-mythical-man-month/

LeFebvre, R. (2024, July 30). *More people are comfortable with AI when applying for a new job*. Lifewire. https://www.lifewire.com/hirevue-ai-comfort-in-hiring-process-8686032

Lepak, S. (2024, October 1). Causes and effects of employee turnover [2024]. *Matter*. https://matterapp.com/blog/causes-and-effects-employee-turnover

Leveraging data analytics and metrics to enhance recruitment and retention. (2023, September 1). IMS People Possible. https://imspeople.com/leveraging-data-analytics-and-metrics-to-enhance-recruitment-and-retention/

Leveraging data-driven insights for candidate evaluation. (2024, October 17). Harrier Talent Solutions. https://harriertalentsolutions.com/knowledge/leveraging-data-driven-insights-for-candidate-evaluation

Loo, J. (2021). *System 1 and system 2 thinking*. The Decision Lab. https://thedecisionlab.com/reference-guide/philosophy/system-1-and-system-2-thinking

Lusty, K. (2022, August 17). Employee engagement & loyalty statistics: The ultimate collection. *Access Perks*. https://blog.accessperks.com/employee-engagement-loyalty-statistics-the-ultimate-collection

Macoveiciuc, A. (n.d.). 43 AI recruitment statistics for recruiters and staffing agencies [2024]. *Carv*. https://www.carv.com/blog/ai-recruitment-statistics-for-recruiters-and-staffing-agencies

Mathieu, E. (2024, March 29). *The service sector now represents about half of employment across the world*. Our World in Data. https://ourworldindata.org/data-insights/the-service-sector-now-represents-about-half-of-employment-across-the-world

Maurelli, M. A. (2020, April 17). *Diversity in supply chain management*. Deloitte. https://www2.deloitte.com/us/en/insights/focus/technology-and-the-future-of-work/diversity-in-supply-chain-management.html

McCartney, C. (n.d.). How to harness your employer brand to recruit and retain talent. *CIPD Community*. https://community.cipd.co.uk/cipd-blogs/b/the_people_profession_now_and_for_the_future/posts/how-to-harness-your-employer-brand-to-recruit-and-retain-talent

McFarland, K. (2016, February 26). *Why Zappos offers new hires $2000 to quit*. RED Strategy Group. http://www.redstrategygroup.com/insights/2016/2/26/why-zappos-offers-new-hires-2000-to-quit

McFeely, S., & Wigert, B. (2019, March 13). *This fixable problem costs U.S. businesses $1 trillion.* Gallup. https://www.gallup.com/workplace/247391/fixable-problem-costs-businesses-trillion.aspx

McKinsey study: Companies make more profit if they have greater diversity. (2015, March 11). Media Diversity Institute. https://www.media-diversity.org/resources/mckinsey-study-companies-make-more-profit-if-they-have-greater-diversity/

McNeel, C. (2024, August 14). *Transform your hiring process by tackling unmanageable applicant volume.* Spark Hire. https://www.sparkhire.com/learn/screen-candidates/unmanageable-applicant-volume/

MHA releases 2022 Mind the Workplace report, finds increasing number of employees have difficulty concentrating at work. (2022, April 12). Mental Health America. https://www.mhanational.org/mha-releases-2022-mind-workplace-report-finds-increasing-number-employees-have-difficulty

Millet, J. (2023, July 12). *How companies and candidates benefit from structured interviews.* HR Daily Advisor. https://hrdailyadvisor.blr.com/2023/07/12/how-companies-and-candidates-benefit-from-structured-interviews/

More than half of employees globally would quit their jobs if not provided post-pandemic flexibility. (2021, May 12). EY. https://www.ey.com/en_gl/newsroom/2021/05/more-than-half-of-employees-globally-would-quit-their-jobs-if-not-provided-post-pandemic-flexibility-ey-survey-finds

Navarra, K. (2022, April 11). *The real costs of recruitment.* SHRM. https://www.shrm.org/topics-tools/news/talent-acquisition/real-costs-recruitment

Nesterak, E. (2021, May 24). *A conversation with Daniel Kahneman about 'noise'*. Behavioral Scientist. https://behavioralscientist.org/a-conversation-with-daniel-kahneman-about-noise/

New research reveals chatbots and conversational AI are an absolute necessity to drive successful talent engagement. (2022, July 26). Business Wire. https://www.businesswire.com/news/home/20220726005482/en/New-Research-Reveals-Chatbots-and-Conversational-AI-are-an-Absolute-Necessity-to-Drive-Successful-Talent-Engagement

Parker, E. (2023, April 4). Time-to-hire metrics: How to streamline recruitment process and reduce time-to-fill. *HireBee*. https://hirebee.ai/blog/recruitment-metrics-and-analytics/time-to-hire-metrics-how-to-streamline-recruitment-process-and-reduce-time-to-fill/

Pestreich, R. (n.d.). The real costs of a bad hire. *Harrison Stone*. https://www.harrisonstone.com/blog/the-real-costs-of-a-bad-hire/

Prokopets, E. (2024, July 19). The true cost of hiring an employee in 2024. *Toggl Blog*. https://toggl.com/blog/cost-of-hiring-an-employee

The real cost of employee turnover. (2023, August 30). *Salary*. https://www.salary.com/blog/the-real-cost-of-employee-turnover/

Recruiter burnout: Signs, solutions, and self-care tips. (n.d.). *Recruiterflow*. https://recruiterflow.com/blog/recruiter-burnout/

Recruitment and retention strategies. (n.d.). OPM. https://www.opm.gov/policy-data-oversight/hiring-information/talent-surge-playbook/recruitment-and-retention-strategies/

Rekha. (2024, August 19). Data-driven decision making in recruitment. *HireWand.* https://blog.hirewand.com/data-driven-decision-making-in-recruitment/

Resourcing and talent planning survey 2022. (2022, September). CIPD. https://www.cipd.org/globalassets/media/knowledge/knowledge-hub/reports/resourcing-and-talent-planning-report-2022-1_tcm18-111500.pdf

Richichi, A. (2023, October 6). Council post: Breaking down barriers: How to combat bias in the hiring process. *Forbes.* https://www.forbes.com/councils/forbeshumanresourcescouncil/2023/10/06/breaking-down-barriers-how-to-combat-bias-in-the-hiring-process/

Rockwood, K. (2022, January 14). *How learning and development can attract and retain talent.* SHRM. https://www.shrm.org/topics-tools/news/all-things-work/how-learning-development-can-attract-and-retain-talent

The role of AI in enhancing employee retention. (2024, September 25). Sales Closer. https://salescloser.ai/the-role-of-ai-in-enhancing-employee-retention/

Ruiz, G. (2006, May 3). *Cheesecake Factory cooks up a rigorous employee training program.* Workforce. https://workforce.com/news/cheesecake-factory-cooks-up-a-rigorous-employee-training-program

Schooley, S. (2024, March 23). *The cost of a bad hire & how to handle poor employees.* Business.com. https://www.business.com/articles/cost-of-a-bad-hire/

Seaverson, E. (2023, December 8). 2024 employee well-being trends. *WebMD Health Services.* https://www.webmdhealthservices.com/blog/2024-well-being-trends/

Sheykin, H. (2024, October 14). Understanding the costs of AI recruitment software. *Fin Models Lab.* https://finmodelslab.com/blogs/startup-costs/ai-based-recruitment-software-startup-costs

Stefanowicz, B. (2024, October 10). AI recruitment statistics: What is the future of hiring? *Tidio.* https://www.tidio.com/blog/ai-recruitment/

Tangalakis-Lippert, K. (2022, April 17). *Starbucks employees face retaliation for unionization in Arizona.* Business Insider. https://africa.businessinsider.com/news/starbucks-employees-detail-pattern-of-corporate-retaliation-for-their-unionization/gg3qjz5

Thammala, R. (2023, May 17). *These 7 companies using AI for recruitment in 2024.* WebPipl. https://webpipl.com/companies-using-ai-for-recruitment

3 times when employees are likely to leave. (2020, February 24). Talent Point. https://www.talentpoint.co/resources/3-times-when-employees-are-most-likely-to-leave

Timmes, M. (2022, June 27). Millennials And Gen Z: Now is the time to reshape businesses to harness their power. *Forbes.* https://www.forbes.com/councils/forbescoachescouncil/2022/06/27/millennials-and-gen-z-now-is-the-time-to-reshape-businesses-to-harness-their-power/

2024 talent shortage. (2023, December 11). ManpowerGroup. https://go.manpowergroup.com/hubfs/Talent%20Shortage/Talent%20Shortage%202024/MPG_TS_2024_GLOBAL_Infographic.pdf

2021 candidate experience report. (2022, November). CareerPlug. https://careerplug.com/wp-content/uploads/2022/11/2021-Candidate-Experience-Report.pdf

2022 guide to candidate experience & must-know stats. (2021, January 30). Clovers AI. https://clovers.ai/resources/candidate-experience-recruiter-guide/

Unleashing AI in Unilever: A HR case study. (2024, January 9). Toolify AI. https://www.toolify.ai/ai-news/unleashing-ai-in-unilever-a-hr-case-study-450814

Wallace, M. (2023, November 8). Hiring outside the industry brings fresh perspectives. *Peak Performers.* https://www.peakperformers.org/blog/hiring-outside-the-industry-brings-fresh-perspectives

Wells, T. (2024, April 20). *An expert analysis of the Chick-fil-A hiring process: What it takes to join the "raving fans" culture.* Marketing Scoop. https://www.marketingscoop.com/consumer/chick-fil-a-hiring-process/

Whiting, G. (2024, March 8). Work-life balance statistics for 2024: A global perspective. *Hubstaff.* https://hubstaff.com/blog/work-life-balance-statistics/

Why reputation matters in recruitment. (2015, December 14). Personnel Today. https://jobs.personneltoday.com/article/why-reputation-matters-in-recruitment/

Why Zappos' training program is insane. (2020, December 4). *Seismic.* https://seismic.com/blog/why-zappos-training-program-is-insane/

Workers are walking away from higher salaries for flexible working patterns. (2023, November 1). Asia One. https://www.asiaone.com/business-wires/workers-are-walking-away-higher-salaries-flexible-working-patterns

Zojceska, A. (2018, December 21). 7 interesting facts about employee turnover. *Talentlyft.* https://www.talentlyft.com/blog/7-interesting-facts-about-employee-turnover

Zojceska, A. (2019, May 5). The ultimate guide for conducting structured job interviews. *Talentlyft.* https://www.talentlyft.com/blog/the-ultimate-guide-for-conducting-structured-job-interviews

www.ingramcontent.com/pod-product-compliance
Lightning Source LLC
Chambersburg PA
CBHW061247220326
41599CB00028B/5562